Paco Rabanne is one of the world's most renowned couturiers. He made his name as the designer of metallic dresses and also went on to produce a series of original perfumes, including the best-selling *Calandre* and *Paco Rabanne Pour Homme*. As well as this his life has been one of spiritual quest and discovery, and he has written many books on this theme.

THE SPIRITUAL FOUNDATION OF LIGHT
Sanctuary of Healing & Teaching
Long Acre Studios, Long Acre, Bingham NG13 8BG

No ....**816**....

by the same author

Journey: From One Life to Another

THE DAWN OF THE GOLDEN AGE

GOLDEN AGE

A Spiritual Design for Living

Paco Rabanne

ELEMENT

Shaftesbury, Dorset • Boston, Massachusetts • Melbourne, Victoria

© Element Books Limited 1999
Text © Éditions Michel Lafon 1999

First published in the UK in 1999 by
Element Books Limited
Shaftesbury, Dorset SP7 8BP

Published in the USA in 1999 by
Element Books, Inc.
160 North Washington Street
Boston, MA 02114

Published in Australia in 1999 by
Element Books and distributed
by Penguin Australia Limited
487 Maroondah Highway, Ringwood,
Victoria 3134

Cover design by Slatter-Anderson
Design by Roger Lightfoot
Commissioned by Ian Fenton
Typeset by Footnote Graphics, Warminster, Wilts
Printed and bound in Great Britain by
Creative Print and Design (Wales), Ebbw Vale

British Library Cataloguing in Publication
data available

Library of Congress Cataloging in Publication
data available

ISBN 1 86204 371 X

Contents

CONTENTS

Introduction

That tomorrow may still hold a promise

This book is the last in a trilogy. In '*Journey*', I recalled my past by sharing my first spiritual discoveries and, more specifically, my belief in reincarnation. I subsequently tried, in my second book, '*The End of Time*', to predict – often pessimistically – what the future might hold for us, by comparing ancient prophecies and the fears of modern scientists.

'*Journey*' came from a natural inner need to write. Perhaps writing was a way of rediscovering some primordial happiness, a nostalgia for the time when we lived in harmony with the Divine. '*The End of Time*' was a harsh warning, although not a series of predictions of unavoidable disaster. I clearly stated that we remain, both individually and collectively, masters of our own destinies. I reminded the reader that the title did not refer to the end of the world, but the end of an era, the passage from one cycle to the next – from the Age of Pisces to that of Aquarius or, according to Hindu belief, the end of the Kali-Yuga age of iron, which is characterized by violence and increasing darkness.

Many prophecies state that this transition will be marked by cataclysmic events and that humanity will be in great danger. We have no choice but to believe that those times are coming, since they are already upon us. Scientists themselves are alarmed: genetic manipulation is happening nowadays, and man now has the means to end his own history. It is no longer a question, as

Paul Valéry[1] said, of individual civilizations knowing that they are mortal; it now applies to the whole of humanity. Nevertheless, as I have already stated, I repeat that this annihilation is by no means inescapable, as long as human beings begin to change how they relate to themselves, to others and to the Cosmos.

The transition into the Age of Aquarius will involve dramatic changes which promise to bring light and peace. Will we benefit from this? We are on the point of moving to a higher vibrational level. Let us remember that since the original Fall, man has been separated from divine light and has become a prisoner of matter. During his slow re-ascent towards spirituality, he must cross seven thresholds, from the most dense to the most ethereal level. After the humanoid stage which was barely above the animal level, came prehistoric man; we are presently on the Third Vibrational Level, that of *Homo sapiens*. When we leave the earth, most of us will pass on to the Fourth Vibrational Level, an intangible world where souls perfect themselves, but are not yet in union with God. That is only attained at the Seventh Vibrational Level. To arrive there, the soul will have to reincarnate for a new term on earth, to atone for all the negative actions which have remained attached to it. If it succeeds in this purification, it will progress on to the Fifth Vibrational Level – that of Paradise. Then the soul will ascend to the Sixth Vibrational Level, where it will encounter the memory of all its past lives. Finally, it will attain the Seventh Vibrational Level, where it will experience the bliss of communing with God. It is indeed a long path, when you consider that we are still languishing down here on the third step of that ladder!

The Age of Aquarius is mentioned in all the great traditions as a period which will mark the transition on earth from the Third to the Fourth Vibrational Level. So the new era will have nothing in common with our present state of savagery! It will be a harmonious age during which *Homo sapiens* will evolve to become *Homo spiritualis*, reconciled in universal Love. One wonders why we make so little effort to gain the most from this promotion! The signs are very obvious; they can already be noticed, if we take the trouble to look. The whole Cosmos is preparing for this vibrational change. By surrounding himself with negativity and destructive acts, man is resisting this change and putting the planet in peril. Why? Make no mistake about it, the Universe will go on without man, and without the earth. Is that really what we want?

In fact, we can actively intervene now, not only to save our world, but also to enable us to live through these turbulent periods more harmoniously! But we must hurry – we are living in a time when the unfolding of events on earth is speeding up, for better or worse. The microcosm of our being is created in the image of the macrocosm. The 'world' is present in each and every one of us. It is, therefore, up to us to act, first of all, on ourselves, in the present.

That is why this book suggests that we abstain from obsessive contemplation of the past and the future. According to a well-known formula, the first no longer exists and the second has yet to happen. Let us not deviate from our present reality, from the moment. We should be wary of the current vogue for celebrating anniversaries which seems to grip governments, institutions and the media. We should banish this unhealthy nostalgia from our mind. The important time, when everything is at stake, is the present. I agree that this is no great revelation, but there are some obvious points which we would do well to remember.

It should be explained that to live in the present is not about indulging in the sort of hedonism which results in the kind of moral laxity and indulgence summed up by the motto: 'Let's enjoy it while it lasts' with no thought for our successors. We should not forget that it took six thousand years to recover from the Flood and that Noah's Ark saved but a few.

One could argue that dying is not such a terrible thing if one believes in reincarnation. This may be so, but if man disappears from the Cosmos, how will he be reincarnated? Those who are shipwrecked by the great storm at the end of time, if they have not evolved during this lifetime, risk being left to roam eternally on an intermediary vibrational level, forever incapable of approaching God.

We should be careful not to misinterpret the theory of the transmigration of souls. Let us be clear that we do not reincarnate to have a better life than the previous one, but to render our karma lighter. It is in the beyond, on the other side, that progress occurs; that is where the reward awaits us, not here. You can be an emperor on earth and yet find yourself on the lowest rung of the spiritual ladder on the other side, whereas a shepherd might be living his last incarnation. The aim is, at the time of our death, to merit passing on to the Fifth, then to the Sixth Level, before merging with God. There, finally, we will find our true joyous home, from which there is no return. So even if we can remember our previous lives, what is important is what we do with each and every day of this new life, making use of this time to improve ourselves, to live in harmony with others and to come closer to God. To remember or to imagine what our past lives were like should not induce us to become fatalistic and lazy – 'I behaved badly last century or I was too happy, so my present misfortune is justified'. That would be a dangerous mockery of the theory of reincarnation. If believing in reincarnation is a refuge for the fearful and masochistic, then I would rather we renounce it. To accept our karma is to know that our destiny, our evolution and our re-ascent towards the light depend on the way in which we live the present.

'Repent, for the kingdom of heaven is at hand,' we read in Matthew 4: 17. This not only means repenting for our sins: it also means 'turning' towards a completely different reality, adopting and practising a completely different way of life. Now there is little time left and the choice has become urgent: will you be among those who will die worshipping false idols? Or are you going to join those who will make the transition into the Age of Aquarius safely and soundly?

We should be careful not to conclude that the only means of

approaching this new life is to shun material things and become a monk or a begger. This is the most common excuse not to follow a spiritual path. If we think that the only choice is between asceticism and luxury, we will soon abandon the idea of becoming an apprentice saint. However, we will see that the sacred texts of all the religions explain that we can progress through every stage of spiritual evolution while leading a 'normal' life, committed to our work, our family and our loves. They provide numerous instructions to help us face daily difficulties. The New Age has not invented anything new – the sacred texts are, primarily, manuals for healthy living, but they also indicate the difficult path to what we know as heaven for those who 'read between the lines'.

Nowadays, these paths should no longer be the itinerary of just a chosen few. The work of alchemical refinement and personal purification is necessary and urgent for each one of us. Certain Gnostic treaties claim that the revelations which lead to union with God should remain strictly secret. They warn against the untimely disclosure of these secrets, even calling upon super-natural forces to ensure their protection. At the same time, Plato's advice to every serious seeker was to abstain from discussing profound questions in writing. Perhaps there were valid reasons for such caution . . . But now we are living through crucial times; all the ancient traditions recognize that at the 'end of time', in the passage from one era to another, it is both permissable and desirable to bring to light certain teachings. A disoriented human-ity has lost touch with truth, but now this truth should once more become operative, and revive the world.

Nevertheless, don't think that I would have the audacity to try to reveal that ultimate truth here, nor would I be presumptuous enough to propose an infallible method to attain it. My only intention is to try to revive the fundamental advice given by the great initiates, which will help each one of us to keep to the path. My dearest wish is that by the end of this book, the reader will feel able to reject both the despair that surrounds us and the attitude which considers contact with God as something desirable but unattainable, save for a few spiritual athletes, sanctified souls or mystics. Potential reunion with God really is possible in our present life and it is offered to each one of us. To those who doubt this or who might hesitate to undertake the quest, the Koran advises (Sura 6: 50): 'Say: I do not say to you, "I possess the treasuries of God"; I know not the Unseen. And I say not to you, "I am an angel"; I only follow what is revealed to me.' Say: 'Are the blind and the seeing man equal? Will you not reflect?' Then we read further on (Sura 17: 72): 'whosoever is blind in this world shall be blind in the world to come, and he shall be even further astray from the way.'

But, once again, it is up to you to choose. Spiritual ascent is an intensely personal matter. If this book makes you wish to set off on this path, it will have attained its goal. If not, meditate on what Hermes Trismegistus said: 'The Work is with you and within you, so that finding it in yourself, where it continually is, you also have it always, wherever you may be, on earth or at sea.'

And the more you pursue that Work, the more the veils of wisdom will be lifted for you. You will begin to find revelatory vibrations within the words of the sacred texts. You may even want to go further, to explore the ancient esoteric interpretations of the sacred scriptures.

Nevertheless, what I propose to do here is not to play at being a Cabbalist or any other kind of decoder of ancestral revelations, but simply to convey some useful discoveries which are the fruits of my long experience.

As Amos said, 'I am not a prophet, nor the son of a prophet, but only a shepherd, a gatherer of figs.' On the humble path of my personal search, I have picked some of these fruits for you . . .

Paco Rabanne

1

Chasing away the Serpents of Fear and Stress

God called to the man, and said to him, 'Where are you?' And he said, 'I heard the sound of thee in the garden, and I was afraid, because I was naked; and I hid myself.'
GENESIS 3: 9–10

Today's world is in the grip of a strange illness. Over the last generation, we have seen the slow development of this virus, which flows through our veins, chills our blood and dries out our hearts. We look in vain for a cure; this sickness is contagious, and spreads like wildfire, causing havoc throughout society. This illness is stress, the most deadly kind of fear.

For a long time, secure in the Utopian delusion of progress and the blissful optimism of 'experts', we lived without that secret terror, even when it was evident in other parts of the planet. The wars were localized (and distant), crises were transient. Even technological and natural disasters seemed exceptional and isolated. Nowadays, however, fear is back with a vengeance. It seems to have reached to the four corners of the globe and nobody can pretend to be immune to it.

Fear of unemployment, fear of foreigners, fear of failure in a competitive world, fear of not being able to cope, fear of not having a roof over one's head, fear of going hungry or without love, fear of falling ill, of dying of boredom, fear of opening up to others, fear of growing old, of no longer being attractive, of losing loved ones, fear of loneliness, fear of retirement or of never being able to retire, fear of the Underground's tunnels, fear of what other people might say, fear of darkness, fear of the younger generation, fear of the Devil, of magic, of fate . . . individual and collective fears, fear of terrorism, of drug dealers, of delinquency, of Aids, of famine, of pollution, fear of the nuclear menace, of the hole in the ozone layer, of genetic engineering, fear of everything.

Nowadays everyone is almost physically aware of the dark cloud of this fear. We are faced with the folly of a world where the main motivations are hatred and greed. Massacres, misery, corruption, crises and accidents of all kinds now fill our daily news reports to the point of nausea. And, lo and behold, old ghosts which we thought had been laid to rest have begun to re-emerge . . . Whole populations are slipping into collective hysteria, as happened in the former Yugoslavia and in Rwanda. Where next?

When man becomes frightened, his aggression soon explodes. This is the fertile ground in which the plagues that now afflict humanity flourish – racism, nationalism, self-obsession, urban violence . . . Our fellow men are the first victims of our growing disquiet, such is our urge to find someone to blame.

Although it has always been with us, today fear is reaching unprecedented heights. According to the Bible, it was the direct result of Adam's fall, when he found himself naked and vulnerable after having eaten the forbidden fruit. In a way, this feeling represents what separates us from our pre-Adamic state; it is what stands between us and that Paradise in which we first evolved, before our descent into matter. Overcoming this inner monster should, therefore, be our first objective in our journey to recover our original equilibrium . . .

And instead, what do we do? How do we deal with the enemy today? We flee from it, we even deny it if need be; but all we achieve by this is to make it even stronger. Stress is that unacknowledged and irrational fear that sticks to us as we fall ever further under its influence. We spend our time fighting a monster which we ourselves have created. Thus we exhaust all the energy we could be applying elsewhere, in real life. This is like the story of Bucephalus, the disobedient horse that was given to Alexander the Great. The King of Macedonia soon realized that the animal was simply afraid of its own shadow. In the same way we balk like restless horses; and the more we jib, the more our shadows become agitated, and so our terror increases. To break this vicious circle, we must call a halt and stop thrashing around in all directions in order to assess the situation and differentiate clearly between healthy fear and paralysing stress.

Very early in life, I experienced a genuine fear for survival, and was thereby preserved from stress in later life. When I was still a child, during the Spanish Civil War, I survived the destruction of Guernica. In 1939, at the age of five, after my father's execution by Franco's men, I fled from shelter to shelter with my mother, my brother and my sister, along the roads of the Pyrenees, at the mercy of enemy planes. When we arrived in France safe and sound, we thanked our lucky stars! Then we endured the German occupation, with the constant threat of betrayal – my mother was a communist – and summary execution hanging over us. In Brittany, every time a Resistance member killed a German, ten civilians were taken at random and shot. When the Germans knocked at the door, our hearts pounded and we were paralysed with fear. We knew an immediate, choking fear, which had nothing to do with imagined stress. We could not afford the luxury of imagining the worst; it was already there, before our very eyes, in the form of corpses fallen by a wall or left by the side of a road. It was our fear that enabled us to hide better, that helped us, that saved us – and we were glad of it. Yes, indeed! I remember my mother sighing with relief one morning: 'We are all still alive today . . .'

Her words seemed unreal to me, but that was what really mattered – the joy of still being alive. If there were only three potatoes to share that day, we savoured them as we would a miraculous feast. The real danger, harsh and immediate, trebled our joy of living.

Since then, each day that passes has been a blessing. Modern stress has, therefore, never affected me. I was amazed to discover it in the people around me, who, being younger, had not lived through the war and who experienced an unease about feeling misunderstood or not finding their place in society. In short, this stress was a luxury reserved for those who, secure in the comforts and delusions characteristic of the period between the 1950s and the 1970s, could afford to play at inventing their own suffering. Today, however, stress reflects some very real fears and affects everyone.

Nevertheless, it is certain that this modern phenomenon of stress will never allow us to solve any personal or global problems. The spelling of this word is very revealing, with the sinister letter 's' appearing three times, as if to symbolize the 'serpents hissing in our heads' which are the product of our own negativity. This is the worst kind of pollution; because it is invisible, we think it cannot be overcome. Positive fear causes a positive reaction. If a worker fears losing his job, a situation which is quite common nowadays, he will try to increase his productivity; or if he is made redundant, he will look for other opportunities. However, if he nurtures a *stressful* obsession about losing his job, his performance will deteriorate, he will become aggressive and jeopardize his situation. As a result, he will feel unable to find a solution to his impending unemployment. Stress is either paralysing and numbing, or else it plunges us into frantic activity, making us incompetent or worse.

Fear warns us, whereas stress threatens us pointlessly. Some people have told me that my book *The End of Time* frightened them. Well, that was exactly what I intended! But do not misunderstand me; by underlining the correspondence between the apocalyptic texts of all religions and the facts observed by contemporary scientists, which describe a world in the process of self-destruction, I was not playing at being a prophet of doom. My intention was to issue a warning in order to provoke a reaction. Throughout this century (although the root cause goes back further), without the slightest consideration for future generations who are unable to speak for themselves, we have ransacked our planet, sacrificed our daily life to the 'Golden Calf', to a mis-conceived notion of progress, to facile solutions, to the accumulation of possessions to which we lose our soul. We should not therefore be surprised if we suddenly wake up terrified at the idea that in our blindness we have sawn off the branch on which we are sitting. I felt I had to alert people, jolt them into awareness and show them the urgent need for a radical change in our behaviour, if the dangers which threaten us are to be averted. This fear, far from being futile, is a sign of respect for the future of the human race. We must not forget that the person who raises the alarm has no other intention but that of avoiding, *preventing*, the calamity that he announces. If he succeeds, his warnings will fall flat, denied by the sequence of events. And that, I must tell you, has always been my dearest wish . . .

But, if this is to occur, we cannot withdraw into terrified expectation. First of all we must deal with ourselves and the way we live. Our lives will, most certainly, be enriched as a result. To lighten our karma does not mean we have to suffer a thousand ills, whether real, imaginary or unconsciously provoked. The wise man is never masochistic nor restricted, but is in fact less strained. To free ourselves from the serpents of stress, the first step towards well-being and self-fulfilment is to stop and take stock of the damage and to find its causes.

These days, we are as afraid to live as we are to die. Stress suffocates our vitality, like a boa constrictor; it infects us and invades our weakened will, resulting in a feeling of impotence which everything around us seems to foster.

Faced with these growing dangers, it is clear that nowadays this feeling of impotence predominates. This is true not just of individuals, but also of whole nations. We all instinctively know we must do something about it, but no one knows where to start, for the difficulties seem insurmountable. Deep down, we are all subject to the law of inertia: we wait for others to take the initiative, while knowing full well that nobody is going to do any-thing and that, therefore, nothing will ever be done. Then what? Nobody understands what is happening any more. The logical link between events is overlooked, and the sources of information have become muddled, unclear and contradictory. Where are the causes, and what are the effects? The numerous interpretations of the same events are overwhelming, and our vision is blurred by an over-abundance of points of view.

In fact, modern man has lost his sense of unity in relation to the rest of the world. The whole of Western civilization has reached a state of extreme mental fragmentation. At first we rendered unto Caesar what was his. Then philosophy and science claimed their independence. Little by little, knowledge became compartmental-ized into countless disciplines – economic, social, scientific and cultural. These disciplines have been further divided into numerous sub-sections which, to defend their own status, have carefully raised insurmountable barriers between them. Modernity has brought with it complexity. We could have simply marvelled at this, for the world's unending variety is the reflection of cosmic infinity. But by becoming immersed in detail, we have cut our-selves off from our original connections with our world. How can we not experience stress when we perceive our Universe as if blown apart by dynamite? Our technical civilization has frag-mented our concept of work, which has become ever more specialized, requiring increasingly frustrating tasks. No wonder people lose their sense of purpose and, consequently, their sense of responsibility. How can we be expected to love our work? Our daily existence is shattered into separate compartments. It is very difficult to reconcile the demands of work, love life, family, leisure and spirituality. How can we hope to feel in harmony with all of these? The only unity we consider these days is an abominable reductionist view of human beings as *Homo economicus*. Man is then reduced to his economic dimension, his spiritual dimension completely forgotten. How can we expect to be happy?

What incredible irony, what guile on the part of history, that we should fall prey to this feeling of helplessness and incomprehension today – we, who for centuries have nurtured the dream of being all-powerful and dominating matter . . . Crimes have been committed against human nature with the best of intentions. In the 1950s, the 'experts' were proclaiming that the man of tomorrow was going to live in an idyllic world created by the machine. Thanks to automation, he was going to be free of degrading work and enjoy material abundance, knowledge and leisure. These wild mechanistic conjectures were quite idealistic, of course, but they were also fatal errors, responsible for lulling us into a false sense of security. These prophecies overlooked what the science fiction tales of the 1930s had already predicted – that the triumphant machine would end up ousting man, who would find himself out of work, obsolete and impotent.

And yet we have invented a wonderful justification for our greedy appetites and predatory instincts. Hasn't God Himself given us the earth to rule? We are, therefore, free to dominate it. This may have been so, but it was to make the earth fruitful, not to degrade it. Of course, certain countries have seen their standards of living and their material comforts improve considerably, but at the cost of thoughtless exploitation of the planet's communal resources, excessive waste and drastic impoverishment of a huge section of humanity, subjected to poverty and famine so that others can prosper. But now the rich are beginning to realize that in this global village where everything is inter-connected, they have exposed themselves to terrible retribution. In the name of progress, technological innovation has, in the space of one century, managed to bleed dry a planet which is billions of years old!

Now, at the end of the second millennium, what can we do to pay for our mistakes? We listen endlessly to the latest media reports about catastrophes brought about by our own lack of foresight. Not surprisingly, we become more and more discouraged.

For from the swollen belly of technology, the first two Beasts of the Apocalypse were born – radio and television. I explained in my books *Journey* and *The End of Time* how these two extraordinary means of communication, both with such great potential, have been debased and dedicated to the corruption of souls. The number of the Beast, 666, in St John's Revelation was, let us not forget, the frequency of the first short-wave radio in the United States. As for television, it is that Beast which 'has the power to animate the image, to make it talk', as St John tell us,

Today's media is both the best guard dog and the most beautiful herald of the cult of the Golden Calf. It controls populations by manipulating them with ostensibly impartial information, mesmerizing them with mind-numbing entertainment, and analyzing them with audience ratings and opinion polls. This unprecedented way of conditioning, once the preserve of powerful institutions such as school, army or church, is now far more subtle, thanks to the development of computers and numerous other technologies. These new methods are astute and much more efficient. At one time people were free during their leisure time, albeit briefly. Today, we have increased access to leisure, but this is completely under the control of the vast domain of the services industry – organized travel, theme parks, solitary video games. Yet, we never find true joy in these, only simple amusement in the sense that Pascal[2] meant. How can we avoid feeling frightened when we see humanity deny its responsibility and plunge into frenetic forgetfulness in this way?

The world described by George Orwell in his classic book, *1984*, seems gentle and slightly old-fashioned compared to the inferno of electronic and mental surveillance to which we are subjected. For example, it has been calculated that by the age of twelve, a child will already have been exposed to hundreds of thousands of advertising messages. Little by little, these messages impose a certain vision of the world on us, establishing the concept of what is true, good and beautiful. These pseudo-criteria are based on in-depth study of our lowest instincts, such as the need to dominate, selfishness, sexual appetites . . . This is clearly all orchestrated, and nothing is left to chance. Groups of experts of every kind – statisticians, sociologists, psychoanalysts, linguists and ethnologists – scrutinize the most minute details of our behaviour, with the aim of exploiting our vulnerability. There are, for example, machines that can precisely discern where our eyes first focus when we look at an advertisement poster or a supermarket shelf. Hidden behind the plate glass of consumer outlets, or through cameras attached to concealed monitors, the experts home in on our weaknesses and analyze our desires, so as to be able to influence us better. Already in the United States, there is a gadget that can link the TV remote control to the viewer's credit card. Man no longer exists: he is reduced to consumer or user. The image has been given life and we are 'marked on the forehead and on the hand with the sign of the Beast'.

However, it is futile to blame the media, for the true cause of our conditioning is that we allow ourselves to be conditioned! We have lost not only our sense of the unity of the world, but also that of our own self. God in His infinite mercy granted us free will, yet we have allowed ourselves to be manipulated by a cathode ray tube. And by a barrage of publicity, which compels us to live up to a stereotyped image, whatever the cost. We have to learn how to re-centre ourselves, to recontact our inner truths, and no longer to submit to everything and anything. For the tragic split between the 'social' individual and his true self is also a source of stress. Fashion items, the rituals of sport, the worship of pop or film stars, the need to read the latest pulp fiction or to buy the latest gadget, expressing fashionable opinions – this is no longer a mere desire to be 'trendy', but a suicidal herd-instinct on a global level! As far as I am concerned, I have been preaching non-conformism in *haute couture* for a long time and feel I no longer have to proclaim it. It isn't a case of being deliberately provocative, so much as realizing that imitating others does not lessen stress but always means giving up one's freedom. Someone once said jokingly that to insist on being trendy – 'in the wind' as the French say – means to choose the destiny of a dead leaf. Let us not confuse our spiritual desire for union with God with this ridiculous herd-instinct. We must remember that by following the herd, we end up by becoming the opposite of what we truly are. This loss of identity is obviously the source of our feelings of unease.

We must, at all costs, find our true selves and be calm, avoid fragmentation, escape from the growing madness of always want-ing more, desiring 'the latest' because 'it's just come out'. Fashions come and go at a frenetic pace. We no longer love; we have fads. And then we immediately destroy our old idols. Is this a kind of bulimia, a greed for pleasure, or an inability to blot out the profound boredom that comes from our spiritual emptiness?

To complain all the time is of no use whatsoever and does not appease our instinctive fear. Modern man's discontentment echoes Job's laments: 'For my sighing comes as my bread, and my groanings are poured out like water . . . I am not at ease, nor am I quiet; I have no rest; but trouble comes.' Nevertheless, Job was addressing God! The Divine is the only real source of hope as far as our frustrations are concerned. To complain to one's fellow men is of no use 'The worst,' said Alain[3], 'is that this illness is like spiritual cholera, highly contagious . . . So moaning and whining soon becomes a kind of established dogma which is promptly assimilated as good manners.' It is also true that it is not only external circumstances that generate stress. We make it ourselves, we nurture it, we encourage it, as if grumbling has become the only way of relating to others . . .

Make no mistake about it, this age of communication is a time when people no longer communicate! We avoid eye contact, and smiling at a stranger seems improper, even dangerous; we adopt defensive postures as we hurry along streets and through shops, occasionally meeting the questioning gaze of another or the lost stare of some social outcast that makes us feel guilty and want to run away. We meet people without really welcoming them, without giving them our full attention because we are imprisoned by our self-centred worries. Our clothes, our pastimes and our fads help us merge into the crowd, but paradoxically this does not inspire us with the slightest feeling of sameness, much less brotherhood. Following in the steps of the great initiates, this book suggests that we would do well to abandon this fear of the 'other', and re-establish our relationship to the rest of humanity and to know how to make use of love. Otherwise, we will be left only with ultra-modern solitude, which is far from being a solution.

Modern man dreads being conspicuous, and so copies others, but at the same time is suspicious of them, which is another paradox! Many people imagine that they can protect themselves from stress by retiring into their shell. Through solitude, it is possible to rediscover in Nature the oneness with cosmic vibrations, to become conscious of our connections with creation, and simultaneously to understand that our fellow men, who are also God's creatures, can be like mirrors to us, providing a welcome opportunity to understand ourselves better. At the same time we can replenish our energies in this way. Later on we will see what wonderful potential there is for us in doing this.

However, many people choose to isolate themselves, without practising any kind of creative activity. Do they try their hand at painting, embroidery, crafts, carpentry? No, they prefer to fight stress with stress. Look at the damage caused by video games, which may heighten reflexes, but in such an atmosphere of violence and fear that some 'addicts' admit to having to wait two hours before they can fell asleep afterwards, such is the effect on their nervous system. When we think how habitual stress causes high blood pressure, acceleration of cardiac and respiratory rhythms, muscular tension, skin rashes and a greater susceptibility to infectious illness, it is surprising that some people keep coming back for more. Don't let stress become a drug, for any drug is just an escape. It is high time that we took control of how we use 'progress'.

Obviously it's not a question of nostalgia for Neanderthal times, nor of rejecting all the innovations created by our ingenuity, but we need to make sure that we are not overtaken by the *Machina sapiens*, that the use of machines does not mean the gradual ousting of human resources. We know that tomorrow's machines will no longer just perform calculations more quickly than humans, but will be 'animated' by their own powers of reasoning, their own way of thinking. They can certainly offer great services to science, but only so long as man remains master of his tools, for the good of humanity.

However, we can only retain that mastery if we regain full consciousness of the meaning of life and of our divine essence. Would a divine being surrender to a robot? Once again, we have a choice: either we use progress to achieve general well-being or we give in to the mind-numbing ease of living that progress can also provide. Satan is very much aware of that second option. Satan, of whom we will speak again in these pages, denies us access to the Fourth Vibrational Level, where the scriptures state he will remain chained for one thousand years. He, therefore, uses all his wiles to stimulate human creativity, but corrupts its results. Because of Satan, technological developments will very soon allow a third Beast, with implacable efficiency, to surpass radio and television. During a recent trip to the United States, I had the opportunity to see this new invention which enables its operator (perhaps you, tomorrow?) to project himself into an entirely imaginary three-dimensional world, as if he were really there. This is a sophisticated form of delusion. Just as we can enjoy and benefit from watching good television programmes, virtual reality can be put to good use. Surgeons will be able to practise operative techniques without harming living things, students will be able to do their practical work on-screen, and tennis players will be able to perfect their style. Unfortunately the actor-spectator will also be able to harm himself with games and programs which give him the impression of being all-powerful . . . for as long as the experience lasts. 'You will be like gods,' whispered the satanic serpent to Adam and Eve to incite them to eat the forbidden fruit and lead them to the Fall. Thanks to the virtual images which will imprint themselves on his retina, the man of tomorrow will be able to recreate his universe, feel objects and believe he really is touching them, and live surrounded by hallucinations. Already in Los Angeles there are pornographic games circulating in which deprived lovers can live out their fantasies directly in the company of computerized ghosts. Tomorrow, sitting before our computer screens, we will be able to visit Venice, decide to go into whatever palace we choose, and so will no longer have any need to travel. Who will be able to resist the temptation? People will lock themselves away at home and treat themselves to cheap travel and powerful sensations – sex, violence and once again, fear. In this three-dimensional game, we will play out our lives instead of living, and we will no longer have any individuality.

One does not need to be clairvoyant to understand that, on returning from these 'trips', the virtual mutant will inevitably find reality hard to bear. He will feel crushed and insignificant and will find himself unable to cope with relationships with others – those whom he cannot reduce to video creatures! He will then long to immerse himself again in the world of virtuality and there will be a kind of decomposition of that person's psychology. All the potential contained in that human being will be absorbed by non-existent fantasies.

Will we then complete the cycle of our self-destruction? At the moment of our incarnation on earth, the soul is divided in half (male/female), then it becomes prisoner of our dualistic thinking (rational/irrational), cut in pieces by the jigsaw of knowledge, fragmented by a standardized society, dispossessed by technology and finally sucked in by unreality. The question is, will man then become prey to diabolic dictators who know how to take advantage of his loss of identity? Will his defeat culminate in the application of genetics and eugenism, which will be able to intervene even before his birth and determine his viability, his usefulness, his obedience?

I don't believe so. I think that in the event of such things occurring, there will be an extremely violent reaction from the higher powers. I do not believe that the great being which created man, the Cosmos and the laws that govern it will allow such a scandal to happen – using the world scandal here in its etymological sense of a trap into which one stumbles.

But we should be aware that this violent reaction from the heavens may mean the end of the earth and of human beings. Therefore, we must ask ourselves if we should not be thinking about taking steps to prevent this happening. Should we not be avoiding the satanic traps, the deceiving spirit known to ancient traditions, which has created this inversion of values? 'You laugh and you rejoice in the laughter of folly. You don't understand that you have entered the dark regions and death. The shadows have appeared to you in the guise of light,' the apocryphal Book of Thomas tells us.

We should not underestimate those moments when, in the midst of our agitation, in a moment of solitary respite or in the middle of a crowd where we see ourselves reflected, we have a sudden insight and a question haunts us like an old memory: 'Is this real life? Who am I really? Where am I going in such a mad rush?'

The early Christian text, *The Hymn to the Pearl*, tells the story of a prince who is sent to Egypt to search for a fabulous pearl. On the way, the prince forgets his mission and succumbs to material attractions and soon falls into a life of passive indolence. Later, an angel comes to visit him and says, 'Get up and awake from your sleep. Remember that you are the son of a king; become conscious of your slavery and of the master you are serving. Remember the pearl for which you came to Egypt . . .'

That symbolic angel was the enlightened double of the prince, who helped him overcome his slumber. We too should listen to the spiritual part of us which is begging for growth. We should be guided by it, so that we can once again find a meaning for our existence and in so doing find the meaning of the present time.

What we need most to be able to awaken our conscience successfully are authentic guides, real points of reference. For the serpents of stress have fed on the great defeat of ideologies and values, which we have been witnessing for decades. Communism has proved to be unworkable, whereas capitalism appears increasingly to be the driving force behind current world problems. The plan of salvation which will allow the reconciliation of humanity and Nature, will not come from that route.

There were times, in antiquity, when the life of a city was in the hands of 'adepts' or 'priest-kings' – men who put themselves at the service of a higher truth and the common good and who could, due to their esoteric knowledge, act as intermediary between earth and heaven. Today, politicians, even more than the common citizen, idolize money. Caught up in futile argument, all they can think about is satisfying their own personal ambitions which, for some, means giving in to corruption, whereas the more enlightened are concerned about territorial issues. In spite of their claims, they no longer hold the reins: they gesticulate, make crude political promises while showing their own short-sightedness – that is, when they are not extolling racism or ethnic violence. In this world prone to despair, our leaders offer meagre support. This hopeless stress is pervasive among the upper crust of society and spreads throughout the population in waves of negativity, increasing people's disillusionment. To this political failure, we should add the corruption of certain stock exchange and property speculators, those who profit from war and misery, the drug dealers and all those who exploit our planet . . . It is enough to 'make one sick' and indeed many do fall ill, hoping to find a relief from stress by going to see the doctor, who in turn discovers, not without some panic, that he has been left to confront this crisis on his own. He faces the enormous task of finding an answer to the unease of the whole of society. Overworked, he can only contain the enemy by systematically prescribing antidepressants.

Doctors, however, can only treat symptoms, without resolving the deeper problems which lie outside the medical sphere. They can offer palliatives, but are not really able to heal what is, in effect, moral suffering. Where are the men of goodwill who can guide us through the terrifying maze of our anxieties?

In our longing for men of goodwill (we are so naive and in such haste to find quick remedies) we mostly find countless men of ill-will. The exploiters of our malaise fall over each other in a mad rush in which charlatans, tempters and false prophets vie with each other for our attention. We cling to whatever crutch is available – drugs, pep pills, bizarre psychotherapies, clairvoyants, sects which have been transformed into profit-making multi-nationals. Artificial paradises abound, and everywhere we are propositioned with recipes for happiness, just as the Church used to sell indulgences to allow people access to heaven. What kind of salvation can we expect from these illusions? 'If a blind man leads a blind man, both will fall into a pit,' says the Bible.

The proliferation of these false religions is obviously generated, for the most part, by the crisis which mainstream religions are going through. Up until now, religion was able to exorcise our fears. Today, it no longer fulfils that function. In some cases, it has even gone so far as to mislead, disseminating fear and fanaticism, so as to keep people under its control. As for Christianity, in my book *The End of Time* I commented that all religions are, just like civilizations, subject to cycles. After approximately two thousand years, they become fossilized; and historians have shown this to be true. After the cult of the bull Apis, came that of the Ram; we are now at the end of the Piscean Age, the fish being the symbol of Christianity. In its present form, the Christian religion can no longer answer our questions, because it is obvious that it no longer has the answers.

Faced with the disaffection which it has brought upon itself, the Church no longer knows how to react. For a long time now, we have witnessed its waivering between a grotesque hardening of its attitude, such as the dogma of papal infallibility which is an insult to common sense, and ignoble concessions to prevailing hatred. Has the present Pope not stated that the death penalty could be justified 'in certain instances', thus contradicting the command-ment 'Thou shalt not kill'? Incapable of renewing itself, corrupted by business interests, by intolerance and by the love of power, the Church is on the point of losing both its followers and its material goods. 'Who is left among you that saw this house in its former glory?' asks the prophet Haggai in the Old Testament. 'How do you see it now? Is it not in your sight as nothing'?

How did the Church get to this point? From councils to encyclical statements, from theological quarrels to imperialist compromises, the Church has progressively and definitively lost contact with the Spirit, with the power of the true Word. Luke 11: 52 warned the religious leaders of the time: 'Woe to you lawyers! for you have taken away the key of knowledge; you did not enter yourselves and you hindered those who were entering.' At the beginning of time, God showed Himself to man in all His glory. Those who retained an inner knowledge of this manifestation heeded the words of masters, sages and priests. But little by little, we forgot the Word, and the revelations which it contained became obscured. A slow process of degradation set in; the divine message was misinterpreted, then falsified and finally became fossilized by routine. Emptied of their meaning, the biblical verses became mere words, the sacraments and Christian rites just mechanical gestures. The few people who still go to mass do so, for the most part, out of habit, no longer perceiving its meaning. They blindly go to church and leave unchanged, with a feeling of having fulfilled their duty, failing to nurture the seed that has been planted in them.

Elsewhere, 'God's madmen' have become bloodthirsty fanatics, whereas originally they were the great initiates whose folly represented wisdom, a broader knowledge which was beyond the range of common mortals, and whose aspiration was to merge with God.

To make matters worse, people everywhere consider mysticism to be a delirium of the imagination, whereas it is an integral part of our destiny, an ardent desire which lifts us towards God. It is exactly because we have forgotten the divine presence in the world that we are gripped by fear. When the reality of our existence on earth ceases to be understood as the manifestation of divinity, it becomes opaque, unintelligible and inevitably disquieting. When will we regain the tranquillity of which the famous verse in Psalm 23 speaks: 'Even though I walk through the valley of the shadow of death, I fear no evil; for thou art with me'?

To know peace, we have to rediscover the lost key and find the path which leads to the narrow door. There are many who feel this urgent need, for, despite all the brainwashing, man will always ask himself the same existential questions about the meaning of life, if only to resolve the difficulties he encounters daily. When these questions become acute, he will begin his quest, at first secretly. I have seen people go timidly into esoteric bookshops, sidling up against the walls, hoping nobody saw them enter, for these places are often considered traps for the innocent. Whenever the subject of spiritual search is mentioned now, people smile, and yet it disturbs them, as if they sense that it is a powerful and challenging force. Rationalism continues to praise the virtues of 'reasonable' behaviour, suggesting that anyone who admits the possibility that we don't understand everything is immature. Pay no attention; it's a question of psychological health. Carl Jung maintained that there was a multiplication of 'neuroses caused by the fact that some people want to remain blind to their own religious need, due to an infantile passion for rationalizing.' So this immaturity is not as it seems.

Nevertheless, even if one has decided to go down this path, it is important not to take the wrong road. Spiritual seeking is not a passive experience in which we should be content to wait until grace falls from the sky and delivers us from our anguish. It involves real commitment, a certain way of behaving, a determination to go through every stage, step by step and, indeed, even fighting battles. But, be reassured, it is not difficult: the only difficulty lies in accepting simplicity. An example will demonstrate this. All of this process which leads to rebirth is told in detail in the sacred texts, in the clearest possible way. The fact is that for too long now, we have considered these texts as just impressive historical and academic monuments. We believe they tell us about a mythical past, about an inaccessible and distant place, another world bearing no relation to the one in which we have to live and make the best of. We believe they are abstract and dry as dust, whereas in reality they contain everything we need to help us on our path. They possess a practical wisdom that can help us live fully while lifting us up towards God. They are endowed with a true transforming power. The quest is neither linear nor smooth. When we follow the path, day after day, in our most mundane occupations, transformation occurs imperceptibly and ends up changing the way we look at the world and at others, while freeing us from unhappiness.

We should therefore discover, or rediscover, the educational virtues of these texts, and find again the spirit of the Bible. 'Come from the four winds, O breath, and breathe upon these slain, that they may live', proclaims Ezekiel 37: 9. Let us reread the Gospels as understood by the initiates; not those who 'know', but those who have trod the path, in all humility, in all innocence, so as to live better. 'What I am telling you is the spirit of life,' said John. Let us enjoy the edifying advice and the paradoxes of the Buddhists or the Zen adepts. Let us light our path and restore our hope with the radiance of the Muslim Sufis. Do not expect the great revelation to come at once; it will come, slowly but surely, of itself. The spiritual dimension of the sacred texts reveals itself to the initiate gradually, in the course of his quest. To begin with we should be content with the practice, that is, what is in effect 'practical'. We read in the Koran, Sura 6: 48: 'Whoever believes and makes amends – no fear shall be on them.' This virtue is not to be mistaken for religious bigotry, but should be understood in its true sense – moral energy and strength of soul.

Each reading of the sacred texts takes us a step further in our understanding, but above all these teachings encourage us to work on ourselves. We should not forget that, although the psalms, poems, suras, parables, thoughts and chants are appealing in their beauty and their powerful allegories, they also contain useful advice on how to begin to conquer the fear and evil both in ourselves and in others.

It goes without saying that all the work we do on ourselves will benefit us and the world and help reduce stress generally. Louis-Claude de Saint-Martin[4], the 'unknown philosopher' wrote in his book *Ministry for the Man-Spirit*, 'The universe is lying on its death bed; it is up to you to minister the last rites. It is up to you to reconcile it with the pure source from which it descends, by purging it of all the falsehoods which have contaminated it since the Fall. Purify it, for it has spent all its days basking in vanity.'

Up to now, we have only exercised our destructive power, not just on others, but also on ourselves. What if we were to try to become aware of our transforming power, that power which is capable of reintegrating us in the harmony of the Universe?

2

To Calm the Tricks of the Ego, Pacify the Self

The agitated man makes the angels laugh.
SHAKESPEARE

When we examine the enormous pressure which engulfs modern man, we can easily feel overwhelmed by the enormity of the task of confronting the dangerous serpents of stress. What strategy should we use against them? What weapons should we choose? Exposed to the hostility of the outside world and at the mercy of our innermost fears, which are magnified by the serpents' actions, we have gradually lost the direct link which unites us with the self, as well as with Nature and with God. We are constantly lagging behind, 'out of step' with our lives. This expression 'out of step' has acquired a special meaning for me. I can feel and actually see this all around. Human beings are normally surrounded by an aura which is more or less luminous, depending on their spiritual development, a kind of ethereal body surrounding their physical one. Due to a natural gift, sustained by sharp observation, I am able to see these auras. Now, every single day, when meeting people, I can see that their aura has been displaced to the left, an obvious sign of 'uncentredness'. Man has been 'distracted' from his real path, in the sense that he has been taken away from it; he is going 'off the rails'. To correct this deviant behaviour, which has dire consequences, it is necessary first of all gradually to repossess our inner space. We must start by finding ourselves again; an essential step, in fact, for how can we act on ourselves if we remain elusive? How can we hope to change the world if we are not masters in our own house? We should try to find our centre, before trying to harmonize with our environment, with others and finally with God. To give ourselves up to the One, we first have to acknowledge our own uniqueness and then our life on earth will begin to show the effects.

What should we do to begin with? First, there is one obvious way, which beckons like an invitation. Since the source of our stress lies in the confusion and disorder of the overworked mind, we should first try to impose silence on it. In other words, to calm our perpetual agitation, we need to silence that hollow drum which is the 'I', the ego. Our sensations and our thoughts cross and run over each other like travellers in a busy station, frequently quarrelling noisily among themselves, creating in our minds a state of acute excitement that controls our attention. The thick web of our desires and our material worries, the passion for the intricacies of analysis which our spirit cultivates, the obsessive examination of our personal anxieties, the distortions caused by our phobias – all these veils obscure our basic perception of reality, just as the numerous veils of the Goddess Isis masked her divine light. Therefore, if we really want to rediscover and hold on to reality, the first step must be to calm the tumult of our overly intricate mental mechanism, now gone completely haywire, whose faulty cogwheels are breaking down.

Buddha compared the spirit of a confused man to a glass of water polluted by mud. The mud prevents our seeing the clarity of the liquid, just as our mental confusion stops us from recognizing the true nature of our being. As soiled water becomes undrinkable, so is our behaviour contaminated by our incessant rationalizations. We should let it settle, so that the divine purity of spirit can show through.

Nevertheless, we should not underestimate all the obstacles we will encounter. We are confronting not just the mental anarchy of stress and daily dross, but also our concept of reality which is made up of our preconceptions. To illustrate this, we only have to think of our conditioning regarding things such as our nationality, our age or our language, all of which weigh our spirits down. The notions imposed on us by our culture, by class consciousness, by our particular profession, by our false perception of our body and by the manipulations of our unconscious, all lead us to recognize the power of that conditioning and the need to go beyond it. If a single speck of dust can blur our vision, just imagine how blinding these smokescreens can become. We need to go through and beyond them, to discover who we really are.

Our intellectual reasoning capacities, which can be of great use to us, will be of no help whatsoever in our search for inner peace. This search is a venture which involves humility, simplicity and, no doubt this is the most difficult part, leaving behind our baggage before descending into ourselves.

Oddly enough, the 'crisis of values' which the modern world is undergoing encourages us to act in this way. The fact is that we now question our beliefs and our pseudo-intellectual certainties. Initially, this generates some fear, but we are lucky in that it also frees us, sweeping away numerous preconceptions instilled in us from a very young age, or developed later in life from half-understood reading or dubious teachings. Today – and this is one of the great opportunities afforded by the end of the Kali-Yuga era – the distorting mirror is cracking. Thus in simplicity the mind can empty itself and return to basic objectivity, to the pleasure of a direct experience of the world, as opposed to the third-hand emotions offered by the media. All the streams of reason have run dry, and we long for a great torrent of flowing water to cleanse our minds. The moment we stop looking at life through a filter, it takes on new colours, simple and yet marvellous, and the world ceases to be mechanical and becomes truly animated.

To create mental emptiness, to induce silence within ourselves, to pacify the ego – all the New Age manuals recommend this, extolling the virtues of relaxation, which does have its merits, but I believe that its benefits cannot compare to those gained from a meditation with a 'sacred' dimension.

Relaxation aims at releasing tension by loosening muscles; the right arm, the left arm, the legs, until the body loosens up completely, which logically leads to mental well-being. But this pacification is rather like taking a narcotic drug. The point is not to run away from our problems, but rather to get a grip on reality here on earth and gradually become sensitive to a greater reality. It is not a question of anaesthetizing our senses but of refining them. 'They ought always to pray and not lose heart,' says Luke 18: 1. If we are only relaxing our muscles, we might just as well do an hour of gymnastics or go swimming. These activities are highly commendable and in no way opposed to the practice of meditation, but they are not comparable. For it is not just a question of relaxing a little but of fully abandoning ourselves and creating an emptiness to allow higher forces to descend within us. We will find that they will help us, in our daily life as well as in our spiritual quest, when we are mature and ready.

The truth is that to calm the tricks of the ego is not an end in itself, but a stage which it is absolutely necessary. We have to go through it, before going on to the other steps which I will talk about in later chapters. Later on I will distinguish between three types of meditation – one which achieves inner silence, one which asks for protection and finally the meditation which leads to divine illumination. For the moment, we will consider only the first.

And don't think that to achieve silence is all that simple! It is not enough to order the mind to be quiet! This compulsive chatterbox defies our best intentions. Most people who try to practise relaxation on their own complain bitterly, 'I can loosen my muscles, but

I don't seem to be able to still my thoughts.' However, there are techniques to do just that – techniques which every major religion has taught, but which in modern times are considered prescriptive, fetishistic and naive. Nevertheless they are the true basis of meditation.

Meditation is not just about imposing silence on the ego, but about creating a void, which means getting rid of that mud which the Buddha talks about. Oriental sages are very clear when they state that the secret of the lotus flower is not in the mud it sprouts from, but in the rays of sunlight which shine upon it; it is up to us to let those rays permeate our being. In the same way, serenity, joy and the simple mastery of our earthly existence will not result from just going through the motions; it can only come by opening spiritual channels and by allowing higher vibrations to reach us. To create a void is fine, but not just for the sake of building a cocoon. We should aim to be silent, not to become deaf to what goes on around us, but to develop better hearing.

You must realize that it is impossible to do without this mental clearing. It is difficult, of course, but it is not such a terrible thing; in time it becomes as pleasant as taking a shower! And don't think that by calming the ego you will become an indifferent observer to everything around you and that the joy and happiness of life will slip away. Precisely the opposite will happen. For the tricks of the ego which we have to fight against are precisely those parts of us which manipulate reality, or rather which cheat us of reality, falsifying it, using it to set traps for us. Freud said that the opposite of play was not seriousness, but reality. For real joy, real bliss here on earth is nowhere to be found but in reality itself. 'The Kingdom of the Father is come to Earth, but men do not see it,' says the apocryphal Book of Thomas.

That noisy ego (the 'I') which stops us from listening cannot be forcefully muzzled to help us achieve our ends; rather it needs to be cunningly distracted in an almost imperceptible manner. The following preparatory exercises can help us pass from an anarchic state of stressful agitation to a temporary emptiness which will allow our inner reality to expand and progressively reoccupy the forefront of the stage from which it was banished. 'Don't lose the fragment of light which you hold,' said the Muslim poet Iqbal. 'Grasp firmly the kernel of your being. Sculpt anew your ancient form, examine yourself, create a living being. Only a living being is worthy of praise, otherwise the fire of existence is but smoke.'

Does this seem an ambitious plan? Perhaps. But it is the only one available to us, for it is precisely our selves that are the *prima materia* of that transformation. Furthermore, this work soon reveals its benefits. All we need to do is to start and it will not cease to yield fruit. In the *Tao Te Ching*, a guide to the 'Way and the Virtue' written by Lao Tsu some centuries before Jesus Christ, there was an emphasis on what could be adopted as the golden rule for any practice: 'That tree that fills your arms, its principle is a minute seed; that tower and those nine floors sprung from a small plot of land; that voyage of a thousand leagues started with a single step.' Let us start then, let us take that first step. And if, as the Koran states, 'purity is half the faith', let us remember that 'the beginning is one half of everything' (Aristotle). Some of us will travel by running, and others will limp, but everyone will arrive at the end at their own pace.

Now that we have an idea of the general strategy and of what the combat entails, we need to try to determine how we are going to proceed in practical terms. What can we do to bring about silence and be at peace with ourselves? There are numerous methods, developed over thousands of years, and most are contained, as mentioned previously, in the rites of the major religions. Some techniques can seem trivial and some of the advice may appear superfluous. However, make no mistake, spiritual masters have accorded them great importance, no doubt because they were aware that such techniques could provide the beginner with encouragement.

So when talking about the practice of meditation, it is important to start at the beginning, namely the physical position to be adopted. 'To sit in a conducive posture is the true entrance to the practice of Zen,' say the adept monks. And the entrance, as everyone knows, is an important part of the house. To sit properly then is to be already on the path.

That does not necessarily mean adopting the famous lotus position, cross-legged on the floor, in honour of oriental religions. The resulting cracking of joints would risk disrupting my silence! I do not consider myself a 'sitting on the floor' kind of person, but rather one who sits on a chair. By the way, contrary to popular belief, sitting on a chair is part of Buddhist iconography. From my point of view, neither is there any problem with lying down, although of course one runs the risk of falling asleep. However, if you are in bed due to an illness, or too tired to resist the need to lie down, don't deprive yourself of meditation on that account.

My advice is to find your most comfortable position, whether this is in the lotus position, on a chair, or even lying down, whatever posture seems the most natural. I would add that it is important not to copy others automatically, for to begin by adopting an authority other than oneself would indeed be a curious way of starting work on one's own liberation. Our physical capabilities differ according to our own bodies and ages. It would, therefore, be absurd to impose on anybody a posture that could hinder them. We should avoid adopting too restrictive a posture, for it would then become the focus of our attention and get in the way of our concentration.

Numerous false gurus take mischievious pleasure in imposing dangerous physical restrictions – they decree that one must lift one's feet in the air, do a handstand or become cross-eyed while staring at the end of one's nose . . . In all these aberrations, one is effectively searching for a kind of false originality and not transformation. It could be argued that monastic orders advocate kneeling, and even prostration on the ground. This is all perfectly acceptable, as long as these positions are not painful, and above all as long as these postures are not ways of humiliating and belittling the body. I believe that what is important is to rediscover the total pleasure which prayer affords, by making sure that the body is not a restriction, but rather an amplifier. It is not a question of constraining the body, but of forgetting it, in order to liberate the mind on which the work is to be done.

Personally I sit on a chair, arms and legs uncrossed to let the energy circulate, with my feet flat on the ground to connect me with the earth, and my hands on my knees. I keep my eyes half closed for, in order to quieten the ego, one must first outwit it! By closing my eyes completely I would allow my mind the opportunity to wander; by leaving them fully open, I could be distracted by noticing a book on the shelf, a shadow in the garden, a bird flying across the sky, and so on.

I sit leaning forward slightly, so as not to cut off the circulation of the blood at thigh level and, above all, so that I am not tempted to lie back in the chair. Personally I have to control the straightness of my back; I try to relax my shoulders, while resisting gradually slackening my body. I visualize my spinal cord as the strings of a cello or a double-bass. If the strings are too stretched or too loose, the instrument will be out of tune. Little by little, feeling my way, I try to find the right note.

We need to adapt our position to be receptive to what comes from above, as if to show our soul's availability through our body. However, even if we recognize that there is not a single, universally accepted posture, there is nevertheless an important point to observe: the posture must emphasize verticality, or at least straightness of the spine if one is lying down. One must be aware of the spinal column, stretching each vertebra one by one if need be, by making slight movements of the torso and back of the neck, while keeping the pelvis still. Thus we can harmonize the bone structure around which our muscles and our nerves are going to reorganize themselves. We then become really aware of our organs, of our blood vessels, and fit ease with the body.

We cannot renew our energies efficiently if we are not in harmony with our body. Any imbalance provokes constant and exhausting electromagnetic exchanges: the subtle body, the aura, wants to return to its place and finds that it cannot, and the result is an enormous energy loss. Many of our illnesses come from the fact that our spinal column is out of place and does not occupy the centre of the energy meridian. All sorts of ailments can be triggered by this – backaches, headaches, muscular tension, migraines, stiffness and diseased organs. These can, in time, provoke more serious dysfunctions. The basic requirement for good health, if not the cure for all our illnesses, is a straight spinal column. It is around that axis that the kundalini winds itself, the ribbon of energy that links our chakras, like the double spiral that coils around Hermes' caduceus, one of the world's most ancient symbols. If the spinal column is unbalanced, the dynamic forces of kundalini cannot flow freely. When the spinal column is realigned, these forces begin to flow again and tiredness vanishes. The spine then points upwards towards God, a kind of cosmic pillar around which our universe is organized.

This rectification will allow the aura to find its rightful place. It will become progressively more luminous, white or pale blue in the case of people who are very advanced in their search. At that stage, it is necessarily centred. When it turns a deep violet colour, the aura becomes like a halo above the head. We are then in perfect harmony with our inner self.

Beginners may find that, even when they choose the most relaxed position, they have difficulty holding it and may feel pain in their joints. Let us not forget that at this stage we are just starting to put all the pieces back together. Soon you will realize that you are capable of maintaining the position without effort, and eventually it will become quite natural. It is enough to adopt the position just for a few moments to immediately feel the beneficial effects. We experience a sensation of well-being, as if the loss of our physical and mental energy has suddenly been reversed. We are now in a position to go into meditation in increased balance and we are already in better shape.

That well-being will be enhanced by correct breathing. When I am settled, with my spinal energy in full flow, I tackle this second exercise. I start by breathing very slowly but deeply in order to ventilate my whole body. It is an intense breathing, which starts from the lower belly and travels up to the lungs. I inhale and exhale deeply three times, then my breathing becomes naturally shallower, until I no longer notice it.

This last point is important, for any breathing technique that becomes obsessive is an obstacle to attaining inner silence. We should breathe naturally, at first deeply, in order to oxygenate the body properly – our bodies are poisoned by lack of oxygen – then gently, in harmony with the flow of our vital forces. In the book of Genesis, breathing is shown to be the 'breath of life': God blew into Adam's nostrils, and he then became a living being. It is through our breath that we are connected to the divine principle. 'May the remembrance of God be one with your breathing,' said St John Climacus[5], the Mount Sinai monk. Similarly, it is by blowing into their nostrils that the Hindu masters initiate their disciples. And if the alchemists were known as 'glass-blowers', this is not only because they reanimated the fire on which their gold-making potions brewed, but because they breathed wisdom. In breathing, as with sitting upright, we have the opportunity of touching the inner core of our being. This inner core has no use for empty speeches, but, in every one of us, is continuously searching for the Truth.

These preparations are very useful; they get us ready for meditation, in the same way as do the gestures which accompany Christian prayer – hands joined or palms open towards heaven, kneeling, or making the sign of the cross. Unfortunately, nowadays these gestures have lost their meaning in the eyes of the faithful. They have fossilized into mechanistic ritual, far from the sensitive and mystical experience to which they were meant to be a prelude. Some Christians today believe that by rejecting these gestures as meaningless ritual, they are moving towards practising their religion with a greater conviction. In fact, by rejecting these rituals, some Christians today have lost a valuable spiritual aid.

Many people, in fact, no longer know how to prepare themselves for prayer and meditation, because they no longer understand the meaning of these rituals. And they end up by saying their prayers in the same way as they would wash the dishes or do the housework. As vehicles of the sacred tradition, religious rites conceal secrets which need to be revived.

Please don't think I am a fanatical fundamentalist! On the contrary, I am convinced that it is the constraints decreed by men which have caused the decline of our religions, and will continue to do so. Ritual can help our bodies to expand towards the spirit, but prohibitions turn God into a dictator. Let us remember what Christ replied to the Pharisees who were astonished to see him heal a sick man on the Sabbath: 'What man of you, if he has one sheep and it falls into a pit on the Sabbath, will not lay hold of it and lift it out? Of how much more value is a man than a sheep!' (Matthew 12: 11–12). Making the effort to adopt the correct posture as described above is not meaningless formality. On the contrary, we *should* remain flexible – the reed feels the effects of the wind more than the oak.

For the practice of meditation, a certain amount of ritual remains necessary, in the sense that it is better to adopt the same position each time, possibly even the same direction, as do the Muslims who pray facing Mecca and the Jews who turn towards Jerusalem. But we should not approach meditation with the idea that a dogmatic observation of rules will guarantee good results. That would be fooling ourselves. We must realize that such a pompous attitude of formulaic ritual and a desire for quick perfection is just a blatant manifestation of the ego, which is always ready to turn everything to its own profit, even attempts at spiritual development.

I will repeat this message many times throughout this book – it is very important to remain simple and humble. And patient! The novice, awkward, uncomfortable and weighed down with distractions at first, will make progress every single day without even realizing it. We should not say right at the beginning, 'I can't, I don't know how.' Everybody knows how to meditate, for it is simply a matter of waiting, not for instant miracles, but thanks to our preparation, for higher forces to come and enlighten us.

Luckily, there are means of avoiding some of that waiting, enabling us to go forward on our quest. The easiest way is to pray out loud. As with meditation (of which prayer is an aspect), we will distinguish between three types of prayer, albeit in a somewhat artificial manner for they are connected – the litany, the request for help and, finally, the real prayer from the heart, the one which seeks union with God. In the latter, prayer ceases to be a means and becomes a state. But, for the moment, let us look at the litany, which is the first step towards the other types of prayer.

What I call a litany consists of the continual repetition of a formula or a prayer. It has fallen into disuse now and is seen as a rite belonging to another era, rather silly, almost absurd, which only bigots or enlightened mystics would practise. The repetition of ten Hail Marys and ten Our Fathers when saying the Christian rosary must seem to some as the most obvious symptom of a faith which has become mechanistic and standardized, the very opposite of true religious experience.

And yet rejecting such repeated invocation is to deprive oneself of an extraordinarily practical and efficient tool! What better way could there be to imprison our mental side than by repeating a prayer which one knows by heart? Thanks to that repetition we are no longer at the mercy of our mind, which otherwise would ceaselessly bombard us with images and thoughts, good or bad. The Koran says, in Sura 29, 'In truth, prayers prevent us from floundering in turpitude and from committing abominations.' Litany is a form of prayer that protects us from distractions; it channels our attention when our imagination wants to run wild. Even if it remains automatic at first, it has its merits and should not be underestimated. Having centred ourselves and done our breathing exercises, we can calmly recite, for example, the Lord's Prayer. Or we might address the Virgin, or, for Muslims, *Fatiha*, which is the opening prayer of the Koran or, for the Jews, the obligatory prayer Listen Israel.

Recite and repeat. For the power of the repetitive prayer is not limited to containing the mind. The sacred formulae and divine names have a power in their own right. 'All who call upon the name of the Lord shall be delivered,' as it says in Joel 2: 32. In all religions, pronouncing the name of God is the basis of meditation, for it is at once nourishing and healing. To say the divine name is to obtain God's blessing. In the Hindu Japa, one of the fundamental exercises consists of the repetition of Rama's name, or of certain mantras. Those resonant phrases which the master teaches his disciple, when repeated, either out loud or whispered, will activate the kundalini energy. Islam, on the other hand, asks its faithful to repeat verses of the Koran in Arabic, even if they don't understand Mohammed's language. To intone such words is to fill our being with divine energy, to merge with it and be enriched by it. It is not the monotonous repetition which has a calming effect; it is the words themselves which convey divine power capable of wiping out our negative thoughts. Repetition only increases that force. The alchemist, when preparing his great Work, begins by making a series of incantations designed to make the sacred fire descend into the 'athanor', the crucible of transmutation.

By reciting these prayers, whether mentally or out loud, we open ourselves to the transforming power of the Spirit, which gradually pervades our whole being. This 'remembrance of God', is the *dikhr*, the prayer of the Sufis, as defined splendidly by Ghazali, a Persian master of the eleventh century.

You will keep your heart empty, but your attention concentrated on God Almighty. This means that, at the beginning, your tongue will assiduously repeat the name of God Almighty. You will not stop saying 'Allah, Allah!' with an awakened and intelligent attention, until you reach the point where, if you stopped moving your tongue, it would seem that the word continued rolling on it, so great is your habit. You will go on like this until your tongue no longer has a role

33

to play; you will see your soul and your heart transformed by this dikhr without your tongue moving. You will continue assiduously until there be in your heart only the sense of the word and you no longer remember its letters or forms, but only the pure meaning which will remain undetectibly and continually present in your spirit. Your free will goes no further than that boundary. It goes beyond it only to reject without truce distracting obsessions. Then it stops acting. You are expectant, waiting for illumination. It may be as fleeting as lightning, not lingering, then returning . . . That is the way of the Sufis.

Everything is there – the concentration, the repetition, the silencing of the ego and the waiting. In the *Account of a Russian Pilgrim*, one of the reference books of the Orthodox religion, the spiritual father advises an aspiring disciple to repeat 3,000 times a day, then 6,000 and after that 12,000 times a day, the prayer said by the Publican in the New Testament: 'Lord Jesus Christ, Son of God, have mercy on me, a poor sinner.' Of course, the point is not having to practise such a feat, but rather to make of prayer a rhythm as natural as breathing, so that it becomes the nourishment of our being. Then, suddenly, the lips grow quiet and the heart speaks. The Sufis confirm this: 'The dikhr starts with the tongue and ends with the heart.' In the same way as the musician's scales are suddenly transformed into a sparkling improvization.

Nevertheless, while practising our prayer-litany, we must be careful that the repetition does not become devoid of conviction, as denounced in the Bible: 'And in praying, do not heap up empty phrases, as the Gentiles do; for they think that they will be heard for their many words,' we read in Matthew 6: 7. Isaiah 29: 13 puts us equally on guard: '. . . this people draw near with their mouth and honour me with their lips, while their hearts are far from me'.

Gradually, we must try to learn not to hum our prayers, 'la la la, la la la', like a familiar refrain. We should listen to them. Take the Lord's Prayer:

Hallowed be Thy name, Thy kingdom come, Thy will be done [humility, putting ourselves in His hands] . . . Give us this day our daily bread [protect my earthly existence]. Forgive us our trespasses [examining our conscience] as we forgive those who trespass against us [hard work, which we will mention again when dealing with the use of love]. Lead us not into temptation, but deliver us from evil [Satan] . . . Amen.

Everything has been said that needs to be said – so long as we become conscious of the message conveyed to us in this prayer.

Repetition and invocation come first, then the understanding and then the sincere conviction; this is what will prepare us for the coming of the angels, of the great guides and of God. We should put ourselves in a state of 're-collection'. So we need to pronounce and repeat the words. Sura 14 of the Koran says: 'A good word is as a good tree – its roots are firm, and its branches are in heaven.' Thus understood, repetition, which we might have thought restricting, brings us freedom; the litany which we believed to be monotonous leads to a great explosion of joy.

If you are afraid that you may not manage the necessary concentration for this prayer practice, it is possible, even desirable, to use 'props'. These help to create a haven of peace around us and establish contact with the macrocosm. The Tibetan Buddhists use a prayer wheel, a cylinder in which they place a sacred parchment and then spin on its axis. Whether it be the vehicle or the incentive for our prayer, such 'props' can be a great help. The rosary, an ancient tool of Christianity, also used by Muslims and Tibetans, is nothing more than a support for prayer.

I have several objects which I like and which help me to regain serenity. They also remind me of the importance of my quest. If my daily world were barren, devoid of any spiritual points of reference, my mind would no doubt feel more free to interfere with my meditation. If my attention were not supported, the mind's 'little monkeys' would return at once to monopolize my spirit. These objects are just what is needed to put my life back on course. In the Song of Solomon 1: 13 we read: 'My beloved is to me as a bag of myrrh, that lies between my breasts.' Whatever it may be, the chosen object, whether held in the hand or gazed at, spreads its vibrations around us, creating a fragrant atmosphere, charged with energy, reminding us of the divine presence.

Naturally, one must be careful not to become superstitious or idolatrous. But as I understand it, the use of 'props' does not involve such problems; they are used just as a reminder. They are symbols, not magic objects. I keep these items around me and they have no other meaning or value than that which I attribute to them. I personally sanctify them by giving them the role of reminders. In my office, I have a painting of Christ, in a rather naive style. I am well aware that it is a simple canvas with a mixture of colours and of practically no monetary value but, perhaps due to the way it came to me, or because of its strong presence, it has become a useful support to help me maintain my vigilance. The painting is not an idol which I worship for itself, but neither is it just a plain image; it is an icon, a sensitive support to help me reach a transcendent state, an open window between heaven and earth.

I also possess a statue of the Buddha, which was given to me by some dear friends when they came back from travelling. When I look at it, with its smile a thousand times more enigmatic than the Mona Lisa's, I repeat 'I am a buddha'. By doing that I am invoking a state of serenity, which I hope to attain. Such objects are visual references in my life. And if I use them, it's not because I endow them with magical properties, but rather because I humbly recognize that the way is hard and that I need the help these external props can give me.

With gemstones, the relationship is a little different, because they are alive, entities which are four hundred million years old, and if one wakes them, they have astonishing powers, for their vibration is in harmony with the Cosmos. They help us connect with cosmic energies. On my desk I keep a large triangular amethyst which I have energized and which says to me: 'Remember your path; do not neglect it'. But we have to be careful and not fall into the trap of turning them into mere lucky charms. For the novice, or more generally, for anyone whose search must be reconciled with an active professional life, gemstones and other such objects are simply reminders, inviting us to take positive steps to detach ourselves from the daily turmoil in order to re-centre ourselves. The monk who devotes his whole life to spirituality may well need a crucifix for the same purpose. Why should we, who are continually exposed to so many distractions, and therefore susceptible to forgetting our commitment, not need our own crutches? The initial decision we took to follow the path may well need to be revitalized at times and it may be necessary for us to be reminded of our priorities. In Orthodox churches, in front of the icons, a candle or lamp is permanently lit. That flame keeps vigil, and symbolizes the spirit of sainthood, that inner flame which we must always keep alight.

One of the oldest techniques for overcoming the mind involves the use of sound. How can we use sound to create silence? Although this may seem contradictory, we aim to create within silence a neutral vibrational state, as opposed to the tiring, negative vibrations of noise, shouting or crying out. But in fact it is perfectly logical: we fight one kind of noise with another of the same nature, but here we are dealing with an inner noise. It is the principle of the sound barriers which are set up around airports nowadays. The sound which the aeroplanes' turbines produce is the same sound that is sent in their direction, using the same frequency, and this neutralizes the noise completely.

For this technique, I use the famous *Om* of Hindu tradition; which has the same resonance as the Jewish *Shalom*, the Muslim *Salaam* and the name of God. *Om* is the mantra of mantras, the first sound of the Cosmos, perhaps also the last, the *omega*. The *Rig Veda*, one of the sacred texts of Hindu tradition, inherited from their Aryan ancestors, says: 'Whoever does not know the Syllable, which is the sojourn of the gods in supreme space, what can he do with the hymn?'

That sacred syllable purifies the inside of the body and removes the forces that prey on it – desire, violence, hatred – as if tuning a musical instrument. We begin by pronouncing the *om*, first by sustaining an open *a* sound, then developing it into *aum*. The *a* is guttural and should come from the depths of the throat and flow into the *o* with tremendous inner force, resonating in the ribcage, vibrating inside us, then finally ending on our lips with the labial *m* as if closing a door. It is said that God has 99 names, plus one which is unknown, that Great Name capable of exorcizing demons and granting wishes. Could it be that God's name is this vibration, which cannot be written but which has to be endlessly modulated?

'Aaa-ooooooooo-mm-mmm . . .', I can feel the sound making my vocal cords vibrate, filling my lungs, then descending along the lowest part of my spinal column, before being exhaled together with all the stress. Once my inner energies are rebalanced, I feel very far away, as if on top of a mountain covered in snow. 'Purify yourself of the attributes of the self, so that you can contemplate your pure essence,' said an Arab poet. 'The Sufi book is not composed of ink and letters; it is nothing but a heart as white as snow.'

When I begin to gain serenity, when I have exhaled my stress, then I listen. The left ear is alert. All external noises are still audible. I say to myself, 'No, that is not what I want; I want to hear the sounds which emanate from the energetic field just 25–30 centimetres around my ears.' Keeping my eyes half-closed, I focus on my hearing. I am all ears and suddenly there is another sound, that of the blood drumming through the inner ear. It is a kind of whistle, a musical note to which I listen with the utmost concentration. Automatically, my mind quietens down, for it is also listening to that strange and new sound. Little by little the noises of the outer world die down. Only that nearby whistling is left.

I then try to transfer that outer sound to my inner self. Slowly, it penetrates into my inner being and I follow it: I go into myself, and I feel tiny, condensed at the centre of my body. Both my physical and my ethereal body expand into the Cosmos. I find that I am both very small, reassembled in the inner kernel of my being, but at the same time vast, cosmic, in a universal expansion far away from my insignificant little worries.

To create silence is to make one's body an inner cathedral, in which one can experience both the calming stillness of a crypt and the swirling giddiness of a nave opening onto the vastness of the celestial vault . . .

When we manage to merge our inner world with the Cosmos, when our heart becomes like a boundless cathedral, we feel peace and harmony. Then we understand the inscrutable smile of the Buddha, bending over his huge, round belly, contemplating this infinite inner self. Meditation removes that gap – which is a great generator of stress – between what we are and what we would like to be. It gives us back our sense of oneness. By creating a void where stress and fear have no place, we are allowing the divine power to descend into that holy place. We are then filled with shining energy and everything changes. At the end of my meditation, I feel animated by a surplus of energy, ready to move mountains.

Nevertheless, be careful not to upset those higher forces by trying to play at being a miracle-worker! Although I use sound freely in meditation and in spoken prayer, I am very mistrustful of some kinds of visualizations. Without wanting to be as purist as the Muslims with regard to images, I am weary of the techniques favoured by the New Age movement (or at least by some of its offshoots) where matter takes precedence over spirituality. Positive visualization is one of the main themes of New Age philosophy, whereby once in a meditative state, one only has to visualize oneself as beautiful, rich and successful for it all to become a reality. To practise Coué's[6] technique may bring good results in everyday life, but not in meditation! You may well prepare for an important meeting by imagining yourself at your most efficient. Regaining your self-confidence is an excellent start to a self-management programme. You think positive, according to the fashionable formula, and you're quite right. But in meditation, you must, on the contrary, implicitly wait for divine enlightenment, beyond the tortuous and sometimes disorderly meanders of your human thought. If you pre-empt this, instead of creating a receptive void, you will awaken the tumult of the mind and all its ghosts. We cannot calm our inner turmoil through our fantasies. This is a good example of the kind of deviousness of which the ego is capable, always trying to prevent us from letting go, making us want to hold on to our mistakes and our prejudices, which prevent us being reborn.

Celestial energies can only come to inspire us if we have made room for them. When we have managed to calm the activity of the ego, we have to wait and just *be*. Inside us we have created a receptive world. What are we waiting for? We are waiting for the coming of higher energies. We should try not to imagine what they might look like, but we can call on them, hoping for something wonderful, luminous and extraordinary. To visualize would only lessen their impact or distort them. Let us rather keep a respectful silence. Nature abhors a vacuum, above all a spiritual one, so when a mental void is achieved, divine energies descend and assume the form which corresponds to that person's religion. For the Christian, for example, they appear as guardian angels, wonderful shining beings, incredible columns of light. These entities will talk to us; some people call them the 'voice of conscience', but if so, it is our higher conscience. And these voices will tell us extraordinary things, and will guide us as we proceed along our path.

Therefore, we should practise and develop that listening faculty; we will then be transformed. Remember the story of Jesus' Transfiguration (Luke 9: 35), when Jesus went up the mountain with Peter, James and John to pray: 'And as he was praying, the appearance of his countenance was altered, and his raiment became dazzling white . . . And a voice came out of the cloud saying, "This is my Son, my Chosen; Listen to him!" '

When and where should we practise these calming exercises? Ideally, we should do them whenever we have a free moment, for example, whenever we have 20 minutes between meetings, or in a taxi, or on the Underground. Or you could sit on an isolated bench in a park, in church, anywhere where you can remain undisturbed. But this is not always possible. Personally, after many decades of practice, I am able to collect myself wherever I happen be – on the Underground, on the bus, anywhere. One must remember to keep one's eyes half closed, so as not to be distracted by passing shapes or colours. During the day, practise these exercises once, twice or ten times, according to the number of quiet moments you can find. The fakirs in India are capable of creating that inner void while sitting in the middle of traffic, in the bustle of a busy street, with cars hooting around them. A Sufi master once explained that the capacity for concentration 'consists of being so profoundly occupied with one's own dikhr that one can stroll in the middle of a market place without being aware of the noise.'

But in order to do that one must acquire total mastery, which is far from being the case for most people. For those starting out on the path, it is advisable to practise meditation in a quiet room, as far away from external noises as possible. 'But when you pray, go into your room and shut the door' (Matthew 6: 6).

We have seen that constant repetition is a key element to successful practice of these techniques. However, this is rarely possible for the beginner. Muslims insist that prayers should be said five times a day. The Jews follow Daniel's example: 'Daniel went into his house, the windows of his upper bedroom were oriented towards Jerusalem and three times a day he knelt, praying to God and confessing.' At first, we should be content with creating silent space within ourselves morning and night. We read in the Bible, in Psalm 5: '. . . in the morning thou dost hear my voice; in the morning I prepare a sacrifice for thee, and watch'. I believe the morning is, without a doubt, the best time. I always wake up at dawn, just as the birds are beginning to sing, as if to remind myself of the famous esoteric tale by Attar, the mystic Persian poet, in which 30 birds go in search of their king, the legendary bird Simorgh . . . only to discover that they carried him within themselves.

The physical benefits of morning prayer can be seen as the day unfolds. If, from our first waking hours, we let ourselves be attacked by the worries of the day, by the need to hurry everywhere, by anxiety, we arrive at work or even just sit down to breakfast with our family, already eaten up by stress. Morning prayer defuses our concerns and helps us regain confidence.

The psychological benefits of evening prayer are evident. If there is a moment when we must put mental pollution to one side, it is when we are falling asleep. Before resorting to sleeping pills and sedatives, we should do as recommended in Psalm 4: 'commune with your own hearts on your beds, and be silent'. That silence will prevent you being tormented by bad dreams and nightmares, and higher powers will look after you during your sleep.

It goes without saying that these exercises will only be profitable if you stifle, once and for all, that little doubtful voice which whispers, 'All this is useless, I can't do it . . . And what's it all for anyway?' That doubt is the fear in us speaking, and we need to overcome it from the start. I will repeat again and again: the results are powerful and immediate. Surprisingly, stress will gradually disappear, like air from a deflating tyre. We soon notice the difference mentally. Useless negative thoughts vanish; only what is essential remains. Freed from such dross, the mind becomes clearer and more focused. We acquire a new way of looking at the world, finding that everything is interlinked. We realize that nothing exists in isolation, but that everything is connected; that our confused, negative reactions are the source of the various problems we experience, whether in our love life or in our work . . . By stilling the ego, everything quietens down and we can see clearly. We acquire lucidity. Not a harsh lucidity, but a peaceful clairvoyance.

Our inner imbalances are lessened; problems don't affect us in the same way. Yet I have not lost touch with reality. Quite the contrary – I continue to do my work, to create, to give interviews, to meet people, but in a different state, a state of inner peace and acceptance. We also realize that those around us are calmer. Agitated people, who poison their lives with worry, look at us in a different way and say 'It's good to be with you', or 'When I talk, I feel that you listen'. A kind of calm comes over us, like a long river of tranquillity which touches those around us.

Such is the enormous effect of positioning the body correctly and taking possession of one's own mind. And this happens quite quickly once we have overcome the doubting stage. So, why not give it a try? It does not cost anything; even children can do it. Learn how to recover the freshness and openness of childhood. Christ understood this when he said: 'Let the children and the humble in spirit come unto me.'

3

Purifying the Dwelling Place

❧

When the temple is consecrated, its dead stone will live again,
the impure metal will be transformed into fine gold, and man
will recover his original state.
ROBERT FLUDD, 'Tractatus theologo-philosophicus'

Now you are regularly practising these exercises for stilling the mind, you have become absorbed in meditation, and you are already getting positive results. And yet you feel slightly disappointed. In fact, you have reached a point where you feel blocked, unable to enjoy fully the benefits of these techniques. A kind of dissatisfaction resonates within you, disrupting your inner peace. You attempt to tune in and become one with your inner self, but something is missing; you cannot find the right note. The feeling of harmony which you should be experiencing is, in fact, being hindered by a major stumbling block – your body is refusing to join in the process and is lagging behind.

The truth is, it's not your system itself that is a hindrance, but the impurities which are weighing it down. The alchemists knew full well that, in their quest for pure gold, part of the work consisted of carefully preparing the matter on which their experiments were based. By keeping your spine straight, you are already helping to improve the circulation of energies, but there is still cleansing work to be done. All those undesirable substances, such as nicotine, alcohol or other drugs, which flow through your veins, all those toxins which are the result of inadequate nutrition, need to be expelled. When I say that, I don't mean to prescribe anything! But, if you have practised the meditation exercises properly, you will have realized that, in order to move towards real transformation, 'purifying the dwelling place' is an absolute must.

Curiously, most people wear themselves out doing the opposite: they inflict a series of dietary rules on themselves, before even trying meditation. To my mind, this is putting the cart before the horse; submitting to a misunderstood discipline. It is much easier to convince ourselves of the importance of physical well-being once the first steps in meditation have been taken, and once we have become aware of our physical blockages.

The first area to be looked at is nutrition. In the Jewish Apocrypha, Ecclesiasticus 36: 18 tells us 'The stomach will accept any food, but one food is better than another'. Hindu medicine considers food to be a medicine, capable of keeping us healthy or of weakening us when we eat without discrimination. It is up to us to choose.

'Keep your lyre in tune,' said the ancient poet, 'if you want to hear the music of the spheres within yourself.' For the celestial forces to descend to us, we have to be able to receive and house them appropriately. Hermas of Cumae, one of the first Apostolic Fathers, wrote in the first century CE, comparing those celestial powers to young virgins: 'see that these virgins take pleasure in your abode, so remember to keep it very clean! They will be happy to inhabit a clean house, for they are themselves pure, chaste and active. As long as your house is unsullied, they will stay.'

I can see the sceptics smiling. Why should they care about being inhabited by 'virgins' or other celestial forms, when their main concern is primarily their material comfort? And yet, it is those unbelievers who are the first to be disturbed by and envious of those people who are in perfect harmony with themselves, who seem blessed and radiant. So in the name of heaven, if the way of the Lord seems inaccessible and distant to you, something to be explored at a later date, don't block the way for the divine energies in the future by polluting your body now. The body, the spirit and the soul are intimately connected. To take care of our body is to free the spirit from everyday life, and thus uplift the soul, so it may know superhuman joy.

It is not by chance that all religions deal with this at length, giving advice on nutrition and rules for healthy everyday living. Of course, rules vary from one belief to another; they depend on the climate, on ancient traditions and on varying interpretations of the sacred texts. But they make available detailed advice on these matters. Is it too detailed? 'What business has religion to meddle in what I do or don't eat and how I eat it? Let religion speak to my soul, and I will take care of how I want to feed my body,' we are tempted to say. Those who are bothered by such interference by spiritual leaders often readily invoke Christ's famous words reported in Matthew 6: 31–32: 'Therefore do not be anxious, saying, "What shall we eat?" or "What shall we drink?" or "What shall we wear?" For the Gentiles seek all these things.' But, on the other hand, they forget that Christ did not say, 'Eat and drink what you like, and wear whatever you want.' In speaking as he did, Christ meant to warn us not to give in to anxieties about the future, by reassuring us that Divine Providence will look after our needs, providing all that is necessary. But it is our responsibility to make the best of these resources, meaning that we should prepare, physically, to receive the Divine Spirit.

If the sacred texts and traditions mention diet, an apparently superficial subject, encompassing such variations, it is because it holds the key to something essential. In his *Spiritual Exercises*, St Ignatius Loyola makes a point of discussing 'Rules on nutrition to observe in future'. These are not about suppressing natural habits, but rather about becoming aware that daily observation of nutritional rules, while seeming almost trivial, allows us potential mastery over ourselves and over our relationship with the world. If we treat the body so badly nowadays, is it surprising that we are so negligent of our environment? Our attitude to both reveals the same lack of consciousness – we are destroying both, little by little, we are filling them both with deadly poisons and, above all, we refuse to see the urgency of the situation. Nevertheless, we should remember that the Bible tells us to remain vigilant, for God could come into our house unexpectedly, 'like a thief' . . .

What if we were to start by getting rid of those obvious poisons, such as tobacco and alcohol, the toxicity of which is well-established? In *Journey* I merely referred to this 'aberration' which drives many people to clog up their lungs, which are symbolic of our connection with the Cosmos. I was tempted to say that if smokers or alcoholics refuse to admit the great risk they run, then that is their problem and they must bear the consequences, but that would be lacking in compassion. Might it be possible to help those who would like to abandon these habits, and show them a way out? I believe so.

That is where making an effort to pacify mental agitation will prove rewarding. First of all, it is obvious that our consumption of cigarettes, alcohol or other drugs is due to stress, our common enemy. Use of all these toxic substances is basically reinforced by our fear, and in fact those who resort to them are usually well aware of that. It is anguish and panic that make us grab a pack of cigarettes or reach for the whisky bottle. And it is, in fact, to run away from what we see as a distressing or dreary reality that some of us choose to escape into a fool's paradise, even if we risk our lives by doing so.

Unfortunately, it is not enough to be aware of our dependence and its slowly destructive effects to rid ourselves of our bad habits. That would be too easy. This is a tactical error committed by those who make obligatory abstinence an absolute condition for the first meditation exercises. There is a certain logic in that, but it is a fallacy. Smokers know the damaging effects of tobacco, and they know that each cigarette shortens their life, and is a further nail in their coffin; they have seen the shocking photos of lungs which have been blackened and eaten away; they have been threatened with all kinds of cancers; they have been made to feel guilty; they have been taxed . . . All of this to no avail. Why do people put up such a tremendous resistance against all reason? Because, it so happens, that reason has nothing to do with it . . .

By contrast, when through meditation you have truly *felt* in each one of your cells that nicotine is a thick tar which soils the sanctuary of the heart and lungs, and that breathing is one of our main doors to the infinite, you will *want* to renounce cigarettes. All therapists agree that the success of a detoxification programme depends on the firm and willing choice made by the addict. You will take this decision, not to please your partner or to make you feel less guilty, but to allow yourself access to a state of expansion, a blooming which you glimpsed in your meditations. The possibilities of relapse due to group pressure or due to a moment's weakness are, naturally, not to be dismissed, but one fact is certain: the answer lies in the strength of your feelings. Unfortunately, I cannot convince you absolutely, for once again I can only reason in abstract terms. But I can guarantee that, once you have effectively experienced the joy of feeling in harmony with the breathing Cosmos, through your inhaling and exhaling, you will want to increase your lung capacity. Start by looking for that heightened perception of which your body is capable, and you will find the necessary motivation to maintain it.

The same principles apply to alcohol abuse, which clouds the spirit, falsifies our perception of reality and makes us vulnerable to all kinds of negative influences. Nevertheless, I would never ban wine absolutely as it is a divine drink symbolic of initiatory wisdom, as shown in the Bible. But its consumption should be carefully monitored, bearing in mind that our tolerance is much lower than we imagine, and that if the Sufi masters claimed to prefer 'the tavern to the mosque', it is only because they were speaking of spiritual inebriation and not drunkenness . . .

Each time you are tempted to smoke another cigarette or to have one drink too many, take up your meditation position, and practise the breathing and listening exercises. You can thus strengthen your willpower, reduce stress and, above all, revive your body.

We all know that top athletes do not smoke, and that they consume little or no alcohol. Do you really think that this involves making a painful sacrifice? Could it be that they naturally reject everything that might diminish their physical potential? They do not have to resist temptation, nor read medical manuals to become convinced; they have simply acquired a sensitive knowledge of what does not agree with them. We should do likewise. On the roads of India, six centuries before Jesus Christ, Buddha explained his doctrine thus: 'Do not let yourself be guided by your relationships, by tradition or hearsay . . . But when you find out for yourselves that certain things are unsuitable, being false or bad, then renounce them . . . And when you know for yourselves that certain things are beneficial and good, then accept and follow them.' Ignatius Loyola said the same when he asked us to 'examine seriously what is useful and adopt it, and examine what is harmful, in order to eliminate it.' This might seem like a truism, but this saying exemplifies an ideal way of living in complete simplicity. However, we need to be able to make these choices ourselves, according to our own experiences and feelings. The first thing we will discover is that being careful about how we eat and drink does not demand any sacrifice. It is no sacrifice to distance ourselves from a way of life which we have recognized as harmful and damaging to our development. This is actually what it entails to be aware of our physical health: to take care of our body is already to choose, at every moment, the direction which we want to take. It is, therefore, to set out on the path.

Unfortunately for us, we have continuously rejected this path, with devastating results. The first human beings ate only fruit and vegetables, then they began to eat animal products such as milk and eggs, before turning into carnivores. As man became 'civilized', ie discovered tobacco and invented alcohol. Recently, we have gone even further by creating synthetic drugs, and many of us are already eating synthetic food.

How far back should we go in order to counter this negative development? And how should we select our daily food? Most importantly, we need to resist temptation and silence our desires, knowing that the body has a natural tendency towards indolence and immediate pleasures.

Do we have to resign ourselves to strict asceticism? That word makes us shudder nowadays, for it has become synonymous with self-denial and penitence. It suggests a whole series of deprivations, the efficacy of which is dependent on the severity of the process. We know that by wanting to mortify the flesh in order to purify the soul, religious tradition has punished the body, seeing it as the seat of those misleading powers, the senses, the source of all our vices and the main obstacles to our spiritual development.

Furthermore, we recall those pious images of holy men, hermits and 'Fathers of the desert' who renounced everything to go and seek refuge in a cave. A little fresh water, a handful of beans and some roots, plus a cloth around their loins was sufficient for their needs! Such extreme detachment fascinates us, but most of us know that we are not made for that kind of life. We must also remember that most of the Christian saints or Hindu holy men, who thus mortified their body, did so to take upon themselves the suffering of mankind, thus sacrificing their health for a higher cause. Those are rare beings, who are seldom emulated . . .

On the other hand, these days we are witnessing the advent of a new breed of ascetic, less uncompromising, perhaps more refined, but in my opinion, heading up a blind alley. Various gurus, experts in macrobiotics and fanatical ecologists would like us to feed exclusively on plants, grains or fibres, probably hoping to make us return to our primordial earthly state, as it was on the third day of creation. They invoke the example of certain Indian sages or the renowned Essenes[7], of whom it is said Christ was one, all of whom are famous for a very strict lifestyle. Should we embrace Jainism, a particularly strict Indian cult which goes so far as to forbid the consumption of vegetables that grow underground, because in digging them up with a spade there is a possibility of killing insects?

To eat only grain might be adequate nutrition for some sages who dedicate their life to meditation. Perhaps it was appropriate for a time when people led more sedentary lives. But for us, who lead active lives, who travel, who are subject to certain social restraints, such a strict diet is impossible to follow . . . and, anyway, it is completely insufficient for our bodily needs.

The new ascetics remain prisoners of a rationale of deprivation and, therefore, of fear. In their view, the body is no longer a stepping stone towards a higher reality, but a symptom of our mortality. Consequently it is an obstacle that we must overcome at any price. Consciously or not, the new ascetics have reinstated the sin of gluttony, which the early Fathers of the Church put among the first of the deadly sins, before reducing it to the penultimate one, before the sin of lechery. Sins of the flesh were much the same as those of eating flesh . . . For if the monks refuted 'carnality' as an abomination, it was just as much a repudiation of animal meat as a rejection of their own flesh. The mouth then became a satanic access for all the filth of the outer world to enter, reducing us to the level of animals. And so food, which was long considered a blessing from heaven, represents for these deviants a sensual temptation to be resisted. These disturbed ascetics are frightened by the good things of this earth, imagining that the devil has put them under their noses to ensnare them. The result is that these fanatics have become so obsessed by the idea of detaching themselves from the world that any pleasant sensation makes them feel terribly guilty. They eat in order to survive, but they deny themselves anything more than this; above all, and this is obviously suspect, they refute pleasure, . . . and it is by displaying such morbid behaviour that they hope to convince people to follow a path to a better life. We know full well that the initiatory voyage is not a gourmet itinerary, but presented like that, it is certainly most unappetizing and likely to discourage even the most determined.

The strangest thing, contrary to what such people might profess, is that the major religions have never encouraged strict asceticism as a special path. Before becoming the Buddha, young prince Gautama lived in luxury in his palace in North India. As he found no happiness there, he suddenly renounced everything to submit for years to the most terrible deprivations, before finally realizing that asceticism, in itself, leads nowhere and that physical suffering is not necessary for the spiritual awakening of the human being. As far as Buddhism is concerned, one can take refuge in the desert and still entertain impure thoughts, just as one can live in a town and remain pure. The same concept exists in Islam; the Prophet never formally encouraged monastic life and its deprivations.

As far as we are concerned, we must be wary of taking extreme measures regarding food or any other area of life. When we are dealing with rules for a healthier life, prohibition usually has the opposite of the desired effect. An enforced diet tends to become a kind of prison, inhibiting the individual. Unfortunately, many people still try to get rid of their bad nutritional habits by taking radical steps, for example, by adopting strict vegetarianism. They often become bigoted and aggressive in their preaching. Without realizing it, they have become caught up in a trap. Absolute refusal to eat any kind of appetizing fish or meat dish leads to a nihilism which is just as dangerous as the anarchy of excess. Let's not fall prey to these grotesque practices encouraged by certain sects. If you feel your diet is an unbearable restriction, give it up! I can guarantee that it is not the right way to go about things. We do not free ourselves from a desire by saying 'I do not want to think about that'. We risk burying it deep within us where it will ferment and decay. What is the use of getting rid of a bad habit, if we are going to spend our time regretting it? We should try to change things slowly, naturally, happily, because we have realized that they are useless or harmful. But if one day we suddenly feel a great urge to eat a certain dish, why should we deprive ourselves? To avoid excess does not mean that we have to avoid festive occasions and be miserable. To honour a friend or a relative, and to commune with others in the joyful sharing of a meal is a blessing.

I wonder if some people's dietary fundamentalism is simply over-enthusiasm on the part of newcomers to this discipline. We all know that excitement is not conducive to clear-thinking. What these extremists are doing is to turn their new passion into what is really an antidote to passion in general. They don't see that it is as easy to become attached to this type of rigorous practice, as it is to any other deviance or false doctrine. When will we understand that radically changing our way of eating or dressing is not enough for a real transformation to take place? If our search transforms us into freaks, it has most certainly missed the point.

Furthermore, not only does this approach prove to be sterile, but it may well have unpleasant consequences. In the shorter or longer term, our bodies will suffer the backlash of the violence inflicted by these radical diets. That is an irrevocable universal law. The shock of this backlash can be violent, just as in the Basque game of *pelota*, where a ball is hit against a wall and it bounces back at twice the speed. The deprivations and the repressed desires we impose on ourselves end up gnawing away at us from the inside and causing grave illnesses. Lao Tsu warns, 'By standing repeatedly on tiptoe, you lose your balance.'

We need to proceed cautiously and avoid filling our daily life with absurd rules. We might be surprised to learn that Islam, generally cautious in matters of food, in fact preaches an ethic of moderation, which is common to all the major religions. 'Do not declare illicit the good things which God has rendered lawful for you and do not commit excesses, for God does not like those who transgress the limits.' In Sura 5 of the Koran, entitled 'The Table', one reads these comforting words: 'God does not desire to make any impediment for you; but He desires to purify you, and that He may complete His blessing upon you; haply you will be thankful.'

And two verses before that: 'They will question thee what is permitted them. Say: The good things are permitted you.'

But be warned, do not misinterpret these statements by adopting a careless attitude. What is 'good and delicious' should be so, primarily for your body. In other words, everything is allowed, but not everything is beneficial. Hence the need to reintroduce a certain amount of discipline. To be effective, discipline must go hand in hand with perseverance, for it is only by the repetition of gestures that good habits can be acquired.

In fact, we should really seek to redefine our concept of asceticism, perhaps by reducing the sacrificial aspect. In Greek, *askesis* does not in any way mean mortification, but rather 'exercise', 'effort' or 'achievement'. The word was first used to refer to the athletes of antiquity and not to emaciated hermits. In many passages in the Bible, the ascetic is referred to as an athlete, or occasionally as a soldier. In this sense of the word, asceticism does not aim at mortifying the flesh in order to elevate our soul. The reference here is to making an effort, to undertaking a specific task which must benefit the body as well as the soul. How can we hope to calm the soul by maltreating the body?

Let's deal with diet like real athletes. Our aim is to develop our physical potential and maintain it at its highest level. This means adopting a vigilant attitude at all times to make the body supple and obedient and not to exhaust it. If we want to forget our body during meditation exercises, we must allow it to function at its best, as freely and calmly as possible. Furthermore, we need to make sure that our chakras function properly, without overburdening them and without creating blockages; for health purposes alone this is extremely beneficial.

Such effort could be said to be in itself a detoxification programme. Diogenes practised asceticism as a way of finding his path back to Nature, thus rejecting the harmful effects of civilization. We should liberate both the body and the soul of everything that might be an encumbrance to them. Then the base metal can be transformed into gold, and man can hope to harmonize with the vibrations of the Cosmos.

While sports training involves following certain rules, the pro-gramme nevertheless needs to be adapted to each athlete. Without being dogmatic, I will suggest dietary guidelines by telling you about my own eating habits. And of course, it would be nice if I could convince you . . .

Very early on, I decided to omit meat completely. To tell the truth, I loathed it anyway, so this was nothing great on my part. Every time I ate meat, I felt a terrible burning sensation in each of my chakras, all along the kundalini. Without being aware of it, I was experiencing the inflammation provoked by toxins on our subtle energetic centres.

Today my diet is, therefore, basically vegetarian, but not fanatic-ally so for I still eat fish and occasionally poultry. In fact, the Bible explains the reason for these dietary choices. In Genesis, it is said that plants were created on the third day, that the birds and the marine animals were created on the fifth day, but that the 'various kinds of beasts, small or large, savage or not' were created on the sixth day, which is to say, *at the same time as man*. Therefore, they belong to the same 'generation' and this clearly excluded, for me, the consumption of their flesh.

But, once again, there are no set rules. Although I am convinced that I have attained a certain physical equilibrium thanks to that healthy diet, I would not insist on anyone automatically following suit and changing their diet overnight. We have to find out for ourselves and rely on our own judgement. As far as our diet is concerned, we should feel our way until we learn which food-stuffs do not agree with us, and in what quantity; this will differ from person to person. As it says in the Jewish Apocrypha in Ecclesiasticus 37: 27–8: 'My son, test yourself all your life long; note what is bad for you, and do not indulge in it; for not everything is good for everyone, nor do we all enjoy the same things.'

I sincerely believe that if you *really* practise those meditation exercises, you will find that much of your internal tension is the result of eating the flesh of frightened animals which have been taken to the slaughterhouse. One day you will say to yourself: 'I must eliminate this stress, I'm going to give up meat, gradually, and eat fish or poultry instead.'

This attitude shows a subtle effort on our part towards self-awareness. We should scrutinize everything with our own personal microscope. We should be wary of adhering without question to family traditions or national customs. Food combinations, meal times, the speed at which we eat, etc – none of this should be accepted blindly. We should only do what we know is beneficial to us. We will then be able to adapt our diet to our individual needs and freely renounce certain things, without feeling that we are being restricted.

Here again, I must insist that this be done gradually. Beginners who try to go too quickly are like stokers putting too much coal into their engine, causing dangerous overheating. They 'burn up their karma' with great spadefuls. As far as we are concerned, we should take care and practise the kind of prudence which the alchemist Happelius wrote about in his *Aphorismi Basiliani*: 'At first make a small fire, as if you had only *four* threads to your wick, until Matter begins to darken. Then increase it, and put in 14 threads. Matter begins to wash and becomes grey. Finally put in 24 threads and you will have perfect whiteness.'

One of the best ways of purging ourselves of physical impurities is by fasting. Unfortunately, fasting has, like asceticism, become equated with morbid penance and therefore been rejected. Yet, voluntary abstinence from food is a privilege which allows our body to be 'drained' of impurities.

Personally, I fast once a week. I find that it is an excellent practice, a very efficient means of cleansing. On that day, I drink a lot of water, to purify both the body and the mind. I find that I can think more clearly and that it stimulates my organs to function better.

Although not total fasting, the long 'pauses' of abstinence

during Christian Lent and Muslim Ramadan are opportunities for in-depth purification. The principle is the same – the elimination of toxins, the development of a certain physical and moral endurance and symbolically bringing men closer to the angels, who don't need physical nourishment.

Nowadays, the Church has practically abolished these periods of abstinence from food, originally connected with Lent. Obviously, I am not against the fact that these prohibitions are no longer compulsory. But on the other hand, I do regret the fact that we have lost the real meaning and, therefore, the purpose of this tool for transformation. In many cases, fasting has not been completely forgotten, but it has been falsified to the extent of being unrecognizable. We know, for example, that during Ramadan, it is forbidden to eat, drink or smoke from dawn until sunset, and that numerous faithful fulfil this obligation, only to gorge themselves afterwards at their evening meals. And if the Christian Good Friday is a pretext to eat caviar and drink champagne, I am not sure that that was the original intention . . . Zechariah lets us know that God is not fooled by that kind of hypocrisy: 'When you fasted and mourned . . . was it for me that you fasted? And when you eat and when you drink, do you not eat for yourselves and drink for yourselves?' (7: 5–6)

Once again, we should keep things simple. Let's not practise Lent as fanatics. If we look at it from a pragmatic point of view, we should ask ourselves why religions advocate these periods of fasting. First of all, so that the faithful may enjoy better health. You don't have the means to treat yourself to a few days at a health farm? Take advantage of Lent, or of Ramadan or of the fasts recommended by Judaism to balance your excesses, and realize that all your gluttony, whether for food, alcohol or tobacco, aggravates your stress instead of relieving it.

Secondly, try to understand the deeper reason for these periods of abstention from food. Fasting for Lent reminds us of the fast Jesus practised for 40 days in the desert, after His baptism. Forty is a symbolic number frequently found in the death rituals of all civilizations; it refers to the number of days that the soul of a dead man takes to depart definitively from his physical body. This 'quarantine' constitutes a transition in the cycle of life and afterlife. It is the number of trial and of preparation. Therefore, voluntary abstention from nourishment becomes a rite of passage, symbolizing 'the death of the old man'. Abstinence is therefore less a synonym for mourning, but rather a joyous mourning preceding rebirth, which is nothing to do with the sad austerity usually attributed to it. Matthew 6: 16–18 advises us not to practise fasting as a show of piety: 'And when you fast, do not look dismal, like the hypocrites, for they disfigure their faces that their fasting may be seen by men. Truly, I say to you, they have received their reward. But when you fast, anoint your head and wash your face, that your fasting may not be seen by men, but by your Father who is in secret; and your Father who sees in secret will reward you.'

Will you be able to practise fasting or deprivation with joy? I hope so, for you will discover that purifying the body becomes truly liberating, both physically and spiritually, and far from isolating you in suffering, it will open you to others and enlighten you from within. Isaiah 58: 5–8 cries out against those deprivations, which are nothing but personal humiliations:

Is such the fast that I choose, a day for a man to humble himself? . . . Will you call this a fast, and a day acceptable to the Lord? Is this not the fast that I choose: to loose the bonds of wickedness, to undo the thongs of the yoke, to let the oppressed go free, and to break every yoke? Is it not to share your bread with the hungry, and bring the homeless poor into your house; when you see the naked, to cover him, and not to hide yourself from your own flesh? Then shall your light break forth like the dawn, and your healing shall spring up speedily; your righteousness shall go before you, the glory of the Lord shall be your rear guard.

Another efficient way of respecting food, and therefore of not absorbing it without consideration, is to remember that it is a gift from heaven. Consequently, eating becomes a sacred act. The wise man gives glory to God also through his way of eating.

The great majority of Westerners live in such abundance that they have lost the habit of giving thanks to heaven for its generosity. Ancient civilizations used to pray for continued blessings from above and present offerings to their Gods. Today, someone caught saying grace before or after his steak and chips would pass for an old-fashioned but harmless fool. Nevertheless, that reverent approach may well have something valuable in it. The Koran (Sura 5: 114–115) recounts how Jesus, son of Mary, addressed this prayer to the heavens: 'God, our Lord, send down upon us a Table out of heaven, that shall be for us a festival, the first *and* last of us . . . Provide for us. . . . God said: "Verily I do send it down on you; whoso of you hereafter disbelieves, verily I shall chastise him with a chastisement wherewith I chastise no other being." ' If we have the right to eat 'all that is good and delicious' it is always 'while invoking the name of the Lord'.

Don't think that I have suddenly become a Benedictine monk! I am not saying that you should mutter some magic Latin formula, eyes piously lowered before your plate, or that you should adopt a devout expression to break your bread. Especially if you're going to devour your meal greedily the next minute . . . I'm simply recommending that we should be conscious of the sacred nature of food. If we do that, we will no longer swallow it like gluttons. We should pay more attention to this nourishment which strengthens the body and becomes one with it.

Why not take advantage of meal-times to recall that everything is symbolic and a manifestation of God? To take a reverent attitude to something as 'trivial' as perishable foodstuffs can seem surprising and even laughable. Yet, the wise man does not let himself be fooled by the apparent vanity of things and constantly seeks to understand the signs which connect him to Divinity. We should make an effort to perceive the substance behind the appearance and to try to hear, everywhere, in the minutest object, be it mineral, vegetable or animal, the harmony of creation's song.

To eat thus becomes an act of participation in the infinite cosmic round, an opening to a higher reality. To ignore or denigrate our physical dimension will not make saints of us. On the contrary, our work consists of reintegrating the spiritual into every aspect of our lives! 'It's not a question of despising things,' said the philosopher Emmanual Mounier, 'but of knowing what they can do for us.' What they can do is to make us receptive to the numerous presences surrounding us which gesture to us from the other side of reality. Guardian angels and celestial guides are all ready to take us by the hand and guide us towards fulfilment . . .

When our intentions are geared towards God, our actions become sources of energy. And by eating in this 'sacred' way, which is to say, being fully conscious of the benefits being granted us, that energy is multiplied ten-fold. The nutrition we absorb is no longer merely satisfying our hunger: it becomes, as Indian medicine maintains, a sustaining remedy.

Therefore, the nutrients which heal the body are a reflection of another kind of nourishment, of a spiritual nature, which fills the soul. 'I am the bread which came down from heaven,' Jesus announced in John 6: 41. 'He who eats my flesh and drinks my blood has eternal life . . . For my flesh is food indeed, and my blood is drink indeed.' (6: 54–55)

From here onwards, the role of true asceticism seems to be not so much to help us to detach from the world, but rather to awaken our attention to our daily actions. What an ambitious venture and how thrilling! To develop our consciousness with regard to all our daily activities, finally being able to enjoy what we have to hand, under our very eyes, in the present moment . . .

What better opportunity to do this than at our daily meals, a ritual we repeat two or three times a day and which represents one of the central points of our relationship with the world? Despite this, most people let these moment pass by, unaware of their meaning. We have all seen people eating in restaurants, with a newspaper propped up between the wine and the bread basket.

How often have we gulped down our breakfast while jotting down the day's important meetings. It is clear that we don't help ourselves in this way; in fact, we deprive ourselves systematically of the great pleasure we could find in these moments.

The rhythm of modern life does not help. We move in a world where everything is available at the press of a button – electric switches, hot and cold water, domestic appliances . . . There's nothing wrong with making our lives easier, on the contrary, but we must recognize that this automation of our life makes it more difficult for us to have the pleasure of performing simple everyday acts of creativity. Why does the fruit picked in our own gardens always seem so much tastier than that bought from the grocer's on the street corner? It's because of the particular attention we give it. We should try to extend that receptive attitude to all the fruits we taste, as well as to every passing moment. When preparing our meals, when we are eating, we should always try to be aware. To rediscover the joy of simplicity, that is our *askesis* – our Olympic training – or rather, our way to the Olympus of the Gods.

A novice once asked a Zen master if he made any effort to elevate himself towards truth. 'Yes, I do make some efforts,' was the answer. 'What are they?' 'Well, when I am hungry, I eat, and when I feel tired, I sleep.' The novice was quite astonished: 'Isn't that what everybody does?' 'With a difference,' said the wise man, 'which is that when people eat, they don't really eat; they think about something else, so much so that they allow themselves to be disturbed from their task; and when they sleep, they don't sleep, but dream of a thousand and one fantasies. That's how they differ from me.'

Through its physical and symbolic aspects, the meal is certainly the best time to discover our 'being in the world'. But gradually, as we develop a new way of perceiving things, we should extend that principle to all our daily activities. Ideally, these should in themselves become a form of meditation. Then we will be vigilant in everything we do and say – while dressing, washing, walking down the street, working, meeting others . . .

Be careful! I don't mean that we should be permanently think-ing, 'I am doing this or that'. Such an attitude would be narcissistic and self-indulgent. We need to be absorbed by what we are doing, like a child becoming completely engrossed in playing, or like the craftsperson who makes exactly the right gesture, precisely and without effort. This is what it means to concentrate on your work.

This does not mean that we should ignore the past or the future; simply that we should consider them differently, always in relation to the present. How can we experience true pleasure in life if we do not learn to enjoy the only reality which is offered us – the present moment? In Pascal's words, 'We never live, we hope to live and are always eager to be happy; it's therefore inevitable that we never are.' As long as we remain incapable of completely abandoning ourselves to the present, our physical and spiritual life will slowly become devitalized. Buddha warned us, 'By worrying about the future and regretting the past, fools grow dessicated like green reeds cut in the sun.' So let's try not to die in a state of idiocy; let's root ourselves in reality so that we can draw on the spring of life.

Among the greatest virtues, together with discipline, patience and generosity, Buddhism emphasizes that joyous energy which transforms each second of life into an enthusiastic celebration. We are intended to be full of wonder. We should try to live out the saying, 'Desire everything you have and you will have all that you desire'. We should learn to *content* ourselves with what we have, with what we do, in the fullest sense of the word. For the joyous heart, the Bible tells us, life is a perpetual banquet. For joy is of this world. Enlightened by a sense of wonder, the ordinary life suddenly becomes more spiritual and more inspired than the most 'intellectual' asceticism . . .

A person of good upbringing is content with little,
so when he goes to bed he is not short of breath.
The moderate eater enjoys healthy sleep:
he rises early, feeling refreshed;

but sleeplessness, nausea and colic are the lot of the glutton . . .
Listen to me, my son, do not disregard me,
and in the end my words will come home to you.
In all you do avoid extremes,
and no illness will come your way.

Ecclesiasticus 31: 19–22

Moderation is the key word, but this does not mean to compromise. For me, avoiding excesses does not mean being wishy-washy, and the diet I advocate is not about 'having a little of this and never too much of that'. That would be a timorous way of behaving, suitable only for the sanctimonious hypocrite.

On the contrary, it is about exploring our reactions to find our system's individual point of perfect equilibrium. In the end, it corresponds to the ancient concept *in medio stat virtus*, virtue lies in the middle way, which does not mean complying with mediocrity but rather finding perfect balance; by rejecting both cowardice and temerity, we are sharpening our courage.

Perhaps the true role of asceticism is to reveal, definitively, difference between the wrong way of making use of things, and the right way, which puts us on the Path. It teaches us, contrary to what we have always thought, that pleasure is not necessarily the same as sin.

If that means a degree of frugality, so much the better! One of the rules established by Ignatius Loyola is as follows: 'In order to avoid damaging our health, the more we place restrictions on normal food, the quicker we will attain the right balance which we should observe while drinking and eating.' We should experiment to find out what is the right quantity for us, but we can be sure that when we find it, it will be well below our normal rate of consumption. The consumer society is precisely about excess and waste! Whereas the Tao makes frugality one of the three essential treasures, along with mercy and humility.

> To be gorged with drink and food,
> To have need excessively fulfilled,

Is the path of brigands.
It is not the true Path.
Tao Te Ching, Ch 53

The squanderer is someone who makes incorrect use of the things which are necessary to life; he is a troublemaker. He is disorderly, and he introduces disharmony around him. Should we be surprised that our wasteful behaviour regarding food has created a global imbalance, both ecologically and socially?

Zen monks follow this maxim: 'Pay attention to the place where you stand,' and I would add 'and to what you do'. This means being in control of our actions, and understanding how things come about. To practise this daily, at an individual level, is to begin to show respect to the elements and to other human beings. It means saving tap water, which we tend to use inconsiderately although we know that water may well become scarce. It means not wasting bread, for it is the ultimate sacred food. It means not leaving lights on needlessly when we know that our abusive consumption of energy harms the earth. Divinity resides also in water, in electricity, in all the concrete objects of which we should make appropriate use by seeking to make the *appropriate gesture*. Whereas previously we thought these things were mundane, we suddenly realize that they are at the core of the issues on which our survival depends. Does this matter not deserve our total attention and our vigilance?

In Tibetan, discipline is called *tsultrim*. *Tsul* means to designate that which is adequate, as it should be in reality, and *trim* means the rule. Therefore, discipline is 'the rule of reality'. To obtain an accurate result, we must act without going against reality. We should act according to what is and change our behaviour rather than the order of the world.

From this point of view, asceticism is no longer a constraint, but a search for harmony with the Cosmos, which involves a regeneration of the body, as well as of our immediate environment! If asceticism was only to do with economy, it would just be about moderating our faults – we would almost have to dispense with our actions to attain perfection. Whereas when we have found the *appropriate gesture*, the act is no longer a fault but an attonement. It is no longer a question of controlling oneself at all costs, but of entering into the cosmic dance by naturally adopting the behaviour appropriate to each situation. The eighteenth-century Cabbalist Luzzatto thus extolled the virtues of the Cabbalah in relation to ordinary books which simply preached moderation: 'The superiority of the Cabbalah is that it states that the acts themselves become good again and are higher forms of attonement.' We have to find the *appropriate gesture*, the one which does not disturb cosmic harmony, and which does not engender disorder, either in our body, in our soul or in our environment.

In the Tarot, the fourteenth arcanum is the Temperance card, considered to be the symbol of alchemy. It depicts an angel pouring pure water from a blue vessel into a red one. The angel is effecting the transmutation of one into the other to create a violet aura, where earthly red unites with heavenly blue.

To purify our physical dwelling place is, first of all, to be careful of what we absorb and the way in which we absorb it. 'First cleanse the inside of the cup and of the plate, that the outside also may be clean,' says Matthew 23: 26. This does not prevent us from equally cleansing the exterior by performing 'ablutions' – an elegant expression for personal hygiene which has passed into everyday language, but which, in the religious sense, means to wash one's body, or a part of one's body, with sacred purification in mind. Water has always been considered the main purificator by all religions.

On the second day of the Creation, God separated 'the waters which are under the firmament from the waters which are above the firmament'. So we have to go through the ablutions (the waters below the firmament) to purify ourselves by prayer (the waters above the firmament). Muslims wash their feet, hands and face before entering the mosque, following what is recommended in Sura 5 of the Koran (verse 6): 'O believers, when you stand up to pray, wash your faces, and your hands up to the elbows, and wipe your heads, and your feet up to the ankles.' We find this practice throughout the Orient; Christians used to do likewise, before becoming content to dip just a single finger in holy water.

These acts are preparations for meditation-prayer, and their purpose is to separate us from our daily life, to calm us, and still the ego so that we become receptive. Total immersion is considered even more sacred and is dear to both Hindus and Muslims (who have named it 'the great ablution'), and it is part of most preparations for initiation. In certain African tribes, the potential initiate has to curl up in a niche behind a waterfall and spend a whole day under the cascade. People came to John the Baptist and 'were baptized by him in the river Jordan, confessing their sins' (Matthew 3: 6). Some Protestant churches perpetuate this tradition of total immersion, whereas Catholics have reduced it to a simple sprinkling of water. In all these cases, water allows us to reconnect with the Divine Source. No magical transformation is expected, but immersion (or sprinkling) confers the strength to stay on the path while relieving the initiate of his faults.

You might say that these are quasi-sacramental ceremonies, which we could not possibly practise in our daily life. I agree, but that is no reason to deprive oneself of the divine benefits of water. Many of us have forgotten how to take advantage of these benefits. For a long time, due to the prudishness instituted by the Church, personal hygiene practices, among other things, were considered an incitation to sensuality, or even depravity, which did not help matters. Even at the beginning of this century, it was common to bathe fully dressed in convents and in religious schools! Even worse, the Church advocated washing in icy water to subdue the body.

Luckily, progress in the field of medicine and prevention of disease has swept away these prudish notions, and both bathing and showering have become part of daily life, although very often stripped of their beneficial and redemptive meaning. We should no longer deprive ourselves!

For myself, total ablution is more than just a moment of relaxation, and much more than a means of ensuring personal hygiene; it is a way of completely purifying and renewing both body and soul. In the morning, like the Muslims, I get rid of every bad dream – often the result of a troubled subconscious – which may have disturbed my sleep and which is still oozing through the pores of my skin. During my morning bath, I enjoy being in blessed harmony with one of nature's four elements. This may appear to be a little too animistic for some people's taste, but that liquid contact helps increase my vital forces when my day begins. I am reminded of the following verses in the *Rig Veda*:

> Oh Waters which comfort,
> bring us the strength, the greatness, the joy, the vision!
> Oh Waters, give your plenitude to the remedy!
> So that it may be a protection for my body,
> and that I may thus see the sun for a long time!

And above all, I pray! Some people sing in the rain; I pray under the shower. I really appreciate that moment during which water shields me from the realities of the world, so that I may be open to inspiration from higher levels, by purifying me, freeing me from stress, so that I may be one with God and renew my energies to face the exertions of the day.

At night, when I wash my body of urban pollution, I also cleanse it from the moral or psychological blemishes that I may have attracted, witnessed or been guilty of. We must remember that our physical body is surrounded by a more subtle body, an invisible, etheric envelope which holds all the good and bad thoughts around us. Water is an excellent way of getting rid of the negative vibrations which imprison us. And it's all the more efficient when we take advantage of those moments in the shower to meditate. While the water pours over your body, washing away all impurities, you can repeat out loud or to yourself this verse from Psalm 51: 'Wash me, and I shall be whiter than snow.' Alternatively, you could recall the promise in Ezekiel 36: 25–26): 'I will sprinkle clean water upon you, and you shall be clean from all your uncleannesses, and from all your idols I will cleanse you. A new heart I will give you, and a new spirit I will put within you; and I will take out of your flesh the heart of stone and give you a heart of flesh.' Once again, everything has been said. Meditate on these words and receive water as a divine ointment that will take away your worries, and gradually feel your stress glide off you, encouraging and heartening you ('heart' in the sense Corneille[8] meant), and clarifying your ideas. Obviously, the Bible's poetry is infinitely less vulgar than my explanations, but it's no bad thing to show that those wonderful sentences can be terribly practical too! Water also makes us a little more generous, when enslaved by the fears we harbour in our '*heart* of stone' which makes us insensitive to others.

Whether considered physically or symbolically, water is a principle of life and, like food, it is a gift from God. 'We sent down out of heaven water in measure,' says the Koran, 'we are able to take it away.' (Sura 23: 18). It could not be expressed more clearly than that: water is a gift from heaven. Let us learn to use it, like all that is offered to us daily, and we will already be much richer.

We should remember, in the short time we have before the millennium, that water symbolizes the means of both our transformation and our renaissance, standing as we are at the dawn of the Age of Aquarius . . . the astrological symbol being two parallel waves.
Healthy eating, joyous discipline, purification exercises – all these practices are going to bring us well-being, and allow us to see the beauty of reality through fresh eyes. They won't be miraculous solutions to our problems, but they do represent salutary training for us, so that we can better understand the difficulties of exist-

ence. To learn temperance for one's body, without depriving oneself of pleasure, which is also a divine gift; to learn the right way of behaving, to be in harmony with our environment and with others – all this is excellent preparation, which we would do well to extend to our social, professional and family lives. Essentially we must cleanse the physical body of its impurities, thereby preparing the dwelling place for the divine hosts who will then come more willingly to help us in our quest.

But I'm sure you are aware that all this cleansing and renewal is not enough to open the gates of heaven for us, nor to ensure an earthly existence which is free of pitfalls. The snares remain treacherous and numerous, as we can read in Psalm 3: 'O Lord, how many are my foes! Many are rising against me; many are saying of me there is no help for him in God.' Our enemies are out there, watching us . . . but they are also inside us.

4

Protecting Oneself from One's Enemies

No evil shall befall you, no scourge come near your tent.
For he will give his angels charge of you, to guard you in all
your ways.
PSALM 91: 10–11

Do you think we are halfway there? Mental turmoil has been replaced by greater balance, the body which had been neglected for so long is slowly being revitalized, and our attention, now awakened, gives new meaning to our daily actions. We have patiently lifted the first veils which separated us from divine light, and we have started what the alchemists called the purification stage of their work. At this stage we find we carry within us noble qualities. And yet, in spite of this undeniable progress, we have perhaps never been in such peril . . .

Yes, we have made space in our spirit and body, but who is going to come and occupy that vacant space? Our guardian angels, our celestial guides? How can we be so sure? Many of us who desire to go on a spiritual journey are held back by this disquieting question – if we do away with our prejudices and our bad habits, what happens then? Will the letting go and the calm achieved through meditation make us vulnerable? Won't we be laid open to external aggression of every kind?

Some people ask me, for example, whether they will not become over-exposed to other people's manipulations? It's true that by renouncing all the defences built up since childhood, we run the risk of being subjected to negative vibrations from a social environment that we cannot avoid. We must not forget that daily life is made up of constant aggression, to a greater or lesser extent. In my work, my travelling, my projects and my creations, I am often subject to overt animosity. Inevitably I am exposed to traps, whether accidental or set on purpose. Of course, I am aware of the growing benefits of my meditation, but how do I reconcile these privileged moments of recentring with the inevitable conflicts of my outer life? By revealing my true face to the world, I take a risk. Matthew 7: 6 says: 'Do not give dogs what is holy; and do not throw your pearls before swine, lest they trample them under foot and turn to attack you.'

The truth is, we are still afraid. A tremendous fear of the unknown takes hold of us. For we suddenly become conscious that to start on this search is not merely a simple and innocent hobby. This adventure involves a deep transformation, and we will be different at the end of it. I must remind you that on this quest, the 'initiates' are those who are on the path and who know themselves as they are today, without knowing what they will become tomorrow. Even if we are not happy with our present situation, we fear the changes to which the journey leads. Even if we agree that the 'old us' must leave, nevertheless the new person and the future appear too uncertain. But is it absolutely necessary to go through this mystical crisis, which is hardly compatible with our social responsibilities, family relationships or even ordinary human contact?

We may feel willing to go some way, but not too far. Most of us do not really want to be like those enlightened beings who proclaim their love of God by beating drums, or those bearded creatures who stand on soap-boxes to harangue the crowds, or those shadowy figures who hover over Allan Kardec's[9] tomb in the

Père-Lachaise cemetery. Others may feel they are not made of the same stuff as St Francis of Assisi who, coming from a wealthy family, sold his father's possessions and threw the money he made from the sale out of the window before retiring to a place of retreat; nor do they have the spectacular humility of a St John of Capestrano who, in 1456, after his conversion during a sojourn in prison, returned home in rags on a donkey, wearing a mitre made of cardboard on which he had written a list of his sins. It is difficult for us to be as detached as St Ignatius Loyola, who stated: 'I prefer to be perceived as a fool and a lunatic for Christ, who suffered that fate first, than be considered judicious and prudent in this world.'

But who says we have to become saints? To approach God directly is their prerogative! We might be better to combine a spiritual quest with the vicissitudes or joys of earthly life. However, at this stage of evolution the initiate would do well to be somewhat apprehensive about others and, above all, about those obscure 'forces of evil' which often seem to hound him, hindering his quest much more than before. Such forces always appear at times of change.

Luke 11: 24–26 confirms that the man who seeks purity is faced with the threat of retaliation from the spirit of evil: 'When the unclean spirit has gone out of a man, he passes through waterless places seeking rest; and finding none he says, "I will return to my house from which I came." And when he comes he finds it swept and put in order. Then he goes and brings seven other spirits more evil than himself, and they enter and dwell there; and the last state of that man becomes worse than the first.'

That return of the 'impure spirit' can manifest in different ways – snags, delays in the realization of our projects, accidents, excuses which can without our noticing become reasons for not making that extra effort which would help us go forward in our transformation. To give a very down-to-earth example, some of you may have experienced being seized by a panicky feeling when you have just passed an important exam, or obtained that job of which you had been dreaming, or just bought the house you had been hunting. Suddenly, when these things are at hand, we are invaded by a terrific desire to drop it all and be carefree again. In other words, we long to flee from our responsibilities. Or we start doubting ourselves, saying 'I won't manage it, I underestimated the difficulties'!

Then we steel ourselves against such thoughts, we learn to defend ourselves, to open up to new opportunities and to go on our way. You must do just that! Before staking your pride in the conquest of the absolute (the absolute is not there to be conquered, we have to earn it), give yourself a rest, in all humility. Learn to protect yourself from your enemies, whoever they are ... You may discover that they are not who you thought and that your best weapons are those of which you thought the least. There is a whole network of efficient means of protection, even against the devil! All the more so because he does not exist ...

The life stories of the great initiates prove that the more we go forward in our inner quest, the more we suffer attacks. St Anthony, St Jerome and Padre Pio are all examples of how one can be attacked by demonic forces. Jesus himself, after a 40-day fast, was tempted by Satan in the desert. But this is not the 'privilege' of great souls – all of us, when we set out on the path of spiritual development, are at the mercy of these negative forces which, with unabating persistence, try to hold us back and restrict us to the material world.

In my book *Journey*, I described how I was attacked by Satan, under the guise of a black mist which suddenly engulfed me, when I was walking in the street. When this viscous cloud touched me, I screamed in terror and it went away. A similar experience happened in Neuilly, when I was sitting on a bench reading a book. I was deeply engrossed in this wonderful book, St John's Esoteric Gospel, and suddenly I felt that a gigantic black wall was gathering behind me. This sinister thick wall came towards me at a terrifying speed. I prayed fervently, in spite of the dread I felt. And the mass of matter drew back . . . Was this a new attempt to intimidate me, to stop me pursuing my work?

When we speak of demonology, we have to be careful, for there is a popular tradition, made up of ancient superstitions, which the churches have widely used to frighten people. Horned devils with cloven hooves, satyrs or vampires thirsty for blood – all these terrifying beings are supposed to come and torment us as we sleep, or to toss us into the flames of hell with their pitchforks . . .

These grotesque images are man-made inventions. The devil does not exist! But Satan does. What is the difference, you may ask. There is an enormous difference. The devil would be a power to rival God, as if there were two masters in the universe fighting over us. Satan is only matter. Matter which was originally created by God and which was, at the beginning, an important part of divinity. That matter is our earthly home, presently situated on the Third Vibrational Level, from which we will free ourselves little by little, to go towards another life, towards the light of the spiritual world. Matter, having been relegated to darkness, conceived a kind of grudge mixed with a certain relish because it had escaped from God. Thus, it became for us humans a dense habitat, heavy and opaque certainly, but at least tangible, falsely reassuring. What prisoner has not been afraid of leaving his jail? So little by little there developed a conflict between the forces of good and evil in humankind. And this takes the form of our waivering between being bogged down in matter (which is the cause of our anxieties) and spiritual development (which is the way out from the hell in which we are living).

That strength and cohesion of matter, and its resentment at being separated from Divinity, shows itself in our human desire to remain as we are, in our ignoring death, in our non-questioning of serious issues such as the meaning of life. All of these are created by what we call Satan.

Satan exists, he is around us. When we incarnate, we enter into his kingdom. When the apostles asked Christ the question, 'Are you the prince of this world?' did he not reply, 'No, the prince of this world is Satan'?

Once again, Satan is not the anti-God, but the matter into which man has been ensnared instead of seeking to elevate himself. And human beings have, by their negative attitudes, encumbered that satanic matter with unhealthy intentions, granting it ever greater power from millennium to millennium. For millions of years now, we have given Satan his enormous strength. We have nourished him with our desires, our wishes, our revenges, our crimes, and with everything in us that is negative. Satan has become rich by amassing our anguishes, our fears and that stress which he himself encourages to increase his domination.

If he is raging now, it is because he knows that we are at the end of the Kali-Yuga era, which means the demise of the Age of Steel during which the devil triumphed. We are going to be given the opportunity to elevate ourselves towards God and to rise to the Fourth Vibrational Level. Satan knows the Cosmos is evolving. All vibrations, all energies are being intensified, and matter itself is going to change. Satan runs the risk of losing his domain. It is, therefore, not surprising that he should be everywhere, desperately trying to keep man under his yoke. For this reason, he will not hesitate to give human beings the ultimate power. But what kind of power is this? The power of self-destruction. Satan drags us down to the lowest levels, and we accept with delight, abandoning ourselves to the seduction of our worst enemy. He corrupts all human activities, through the medium of his agent, money. Its perversion seeps into science, politics, the mass media and each and everyone's personal life.

When Satan tried to tempt Christ in the desert, it was just the same. He took him up a mountain and, showing him the riches of this world, he said to him: 'All this, I will give to you, if you bow down and pay homage to me.' Christ rejected the offer easily –

what would he want with matter and darkness as the master of the Light?

Unfortunately for us, we find it much more difficult to resist temptation. To fight it is all the more exhausting in the short time left before the end of our present era. Satan is sworn to prevent us from escaping his grip, bent on stopping our preparation for the harmonious time to come, the spiritual Age of Aquarius. He will not hesitate to use, in his ultimate battle, the most underhand means. Already the sects are multiplying, false prophets abound, preparing the way for the Anti-Christ, the charismatic embodiment of Satan who will exercise, at the end of the Piscean Age, his false power over the world. Nevertheless, the scriptures state, as I mentioned in my book *The End of Time*, that the Anti-Christ will sooner or later be crushed by two exceptional figures who will arrive from the Cosmos: Elijah and Enoch. These great beings loved God so much that He called them back to Him without them having to experience death or decomposition of the body. These two beings of Truth will come back to earth to take on the fight against the Anti-Christ. A terrible duel will follow, the final fight against matter which will allow access to the Fourth Vibrational Level . . . for those who have not succumbed to Satan's seduction, whatever guise he might have taken when they encountered him.

How can we be part of the chosen? By persevering in the spiritual search which we have started, working on recentring ourselves. I Peter 5: 8–9 tells us: 'Be sober, be watchful. Your adversary the devil prowls around like a roaring lion, seeking someone to devour. Resist him, firm in your faith, knowing that the same experience of suffering is required of your brotherhood throughout the world.'

Unfortunately, perseverance in our search is perhaps the most difficult virtue to sustain because we are on earth and have to live here. Very often, our daily problems so completely monopolize us that it seems more important to resolve them than to climb the steps to heaven. In a sense, it is understandable; we are here to live our lives fully. St Francis of Sales[10] firmly reminds us that God does not intend for us all to become hermits, monks or martyrs. But, if I may repeat once again, our spiritual quest is not incompatible with the 'struggle for life' (or with making a living) that our earthly existence demands. If we have the humility to put ourselves in God's hands, it should not be so that He will do things for us on a trivial level, but rather for Him to grant us His assistance so that our emotional, professional and physical problems can be resolved harmoniously in our daily life. This is what praying to ask for help is. The prayer-litany was to calm the mind; the prayer which asks for help will allow us to find a solution for our present problems or help us bear them. All religions have hymns and incantations the aim of which is to invoke God's blessing or the help of his powerful delegates, the great guides, the enlightened beings and the guardian angels.

As far as I am concerned, I found a long time ago that the Bible's Psalms are a powerful tool for protection, no doubt one of the best that Judaeo-Christians have at their disposal. It seems to me that one can draw from these writings new strength to cope with times of crisis. In the Psalms, God is described as a 'hospital rock', a 'fortress of salvation', 'my shield, my rock, my fortress, my hope, my citadel, my safe shelter, my strength, my rescue and my saviour'. 'Strike your enemy with the name of God,' said St John Climacus, 'for there is no weapon as powerful on earth or in heaven.'

Therefore, we should not hesitate to call on Him every time we need support. And we should work at retaining His attention! When they enter their temple, the Buddhists ring a bell or a gong to ask God to listen to them. This might seem strange to us, but we should insist, again and again without losing heart, and ask for God's help, by praying and praying, so that He can hear us. The supplications of the Psalms (3, 4, 5, 10, 13, 17, 22, 28, 38, 39, 54, 55, etc) are good examples of this:

> I cry aloud to the Lord,
> and he answers me from his holy hill.

Answer me when I call, O God of my right!
Thou hast given me room when I was in distress.
Be gracious to me, and hear my prayer.

Give ear to my words, O Lord:
give heed to my groaning.

Why dost thou stand afar off, O Lord?
Why dost thou hide thyself in times of trouble?

How long, O Lord? Wilt thou forget me for ever?
How long wilt thou hide thy face from me?

Hear a just cause, O Lord;
attend to my cry!
Give ear to my prayer from lips free of deceit!

My God, my God, why hast thou forsaken me?
Why art thou so far from helping me,
from the words of my groaning?

To thee, O Lord, I call;
my rock, be not deaf to me.

Do not forsake me, O Lord!
O my God, be not far from me!
Make haste to help me.
O Lord, my salvation!

Hear my prayer, O Lord,
and give ear to my cry;
hold not thy peace at my tears!

Hear my prayer, O God;
give ear to the words of my mouth.

Give ear to my prayer, O God;
and hide not thyself from my supplication!
Attend to me, and answer me;
I am overcome by my trouble.

And, above all, don't be afraid to abuse celestial patience! Only an unfailing determination will allow you to be heard. Are you afraid of repeating your plea again and again, like a persistent beggar? Then reread Luke 18: 1–5 which tells the story of a judge who, tired of fighting, finally complied with the requests of a 'clamouring widow'. Christ quotes this example to encourage us to be persistent: 'And will God not vindicate his elect, who cry to him day and night? Will he delay long over them? I tell you, he will vindicate them speedily?.'

Don't give up, for in the end you will be victorious, as long as you're patient . . . Prayer has almost automatic results. Remember what is said in Luke 11: 9–10: 'And I tell you, Ask, and it will be given you; seek, and you will find; knock, and it will be opened to you. For everyone who asks receives, and he who seeks finds, and to him who knocks it will be opened.' Therefore, knock and knock again! I can guarantee that your call will be answered.

Practise prayer regularly, with conviction, and you will see miracles happen, as Christ says in Matthew 21: 21: 'Truly, I say to you, if you have faith and never doubt . . . , even if you say to this mountain, "Be taken up and cast into the sea", it will be done. And whatever you ask in prayer, you will receive if you have faith.'

We all know that there are days when, unfortunately, we are incapable of praying: our thoughts are confused, as if something or someone were interfering with us to hinder or divert our request. Nevertheless, it is precisely at these moments that we must persevere and insist, again and again, until we succeed in re-establishing that radiant contact with God. We can't pray? Even so, we must. We should read the sacred texts, word by word, our finger on the lines, like children. We should recite aloud the Psalms (this is recommended anyway, in all circumstances), perhaps even two tones higher than our normal pitch – a technique used successfully in Gregorian chant and which can be found in most religions. Those who hear these psalmodic prayers speak of 'heavenly voices'. For us, when we raise our voice to a higher pitch, it is as if we were leaving behind our mental, intellectual world, to enter the world of energy, of vibrations beyond words, inhabited by the great guides, from whence they will hear us, as will our supreme guide, God Himself.

And I do mean 'beyond words'! We must clarify a few points about praying to ask for help, so as to avoid misunderstandings. I'm afraid that some naive or very selfish people may imagine that they can resort to this to fulfil all their desires. If that is the case, they are making a big mistake. Can we inconvenience the heavenly powers just to obtain a loan to buy a house or to reveal lottery numbers by praying with conviction? In an extreme situation, of course, we can implore God to help us out of a crisis; obviously, if we are in serious difficulties, we can beg for help. But we should avoid formulating what we desire too precisely with our human words and objectives. For, how do we know that what we desire, however ardently, is what is best for us? Mystics have often said that the important thing when praying is not so much what one says to God, but rather what He has to say to us. So much so, that we have to pray 'in His name'. Christ emphasizes that in the Gospels: 'Whatever you ask in my name, shall be granted. He will give it to you.' And each time the Bible asserts the all-encompassing power of prayer addressed to God, it quickly specifies: 'But Thy will be done, not mine.'

We must try to behave like adults: prayer is not a catalogue of wishes addressed to Father Christmas. Our request for help is also a supplication for mercy. How can we know, from our limited point of view, restricted by our present incarnation, what our destiny holds in store for us in order to lighten our karma? Let's not be too precise in our supplications. Let us be content with putting ourselves under divine protection, with presenting ourselves as servants of God, and the rest will follow. In Ecclesiastes, we can read: 'Give me your heart, and the rest I will give you in addition.' And in Luke 12: 41: 'Instead, seek his kingdom, and these things shall be yours as well.' The popular saying goes: 'God closes one door, yet He opens a large gate for you.' Divine powers do not necessarily give us what we ask for, but rather what we need.

We should try not to be too self-centred in our calls for help. Let us pray for those who are close to us or dear to us, or for humanity. We must realize that our prayer-requests will be all the more efficient if we make a disinterested plea for intercession on behalf of others . . .

If that prayer-request is said with the utmost trust, it should be enough to protect us. But do we really believe as much as we think we do? Fear remains; fear of accidents, of failure, of malevolence, of rivals, of neighbours, of evil strangers on the loose, in this world where violence is everywhere. But there is a type of meditation for protection, or rather one which puts us under protection and which can guard us from certain dangers.

This simple meditation can be practised anywhere, whenever and wherever it is most needed – in the middle of a crowd, for example, if you simply want to protect yourself and you don't want people to look at you . . . What you do is to build a cocoon around yourself; you imagine that you are inside an egg which contains your body. Your fill the interior with a gold and pink light, the colour of the Rosicrucians, and you visualize the outside of the egg as a mirror. The miracle works: people no longer stare at you, they can't see you any more. Their gaze and their thoughts are reflected and diverted by the convex exterior of the egg. You can then start to meditate and pray. At any moment, when panic takes hold of you, you can surround yourself with this positive energy, which will protect you from the threatening outside world, fed by childish anguish, by unhealthy films or books.

Women have always known how to use perfume to weave a kind of protective field around themselves. Perfume can, in fact, represent the inward nature of the soul and allow us to perceive spiritual reality or help us connect with the presence of subtle entities. But there are also odours that can provoke the opposite – magical perfumes which can lead us into the depths of darkness. The alchemists knew that there are certain harmful incenses which should be avoided. Be careful with substances offered by the would-be sorcerers who now abound. They may want to sell you harmful ointments, with the promise that these will bring your loved one back or help you defeat your rivals. It's safer to buy a normal scent, one which simply makes you feel good . . . Beware! Protecting oneself should never mean harming others. This is always severely punished.

To overcome an adversary, there are simple, eternal formulae, or objects such as an image or a holy icon. These can reassure us and repel negative vibrations. They erect a powerful barrier against forces of evil which come to attack us. For the novice, peril will present itself mainly as outward danger. This isn't always the case, but we must recognize that it can come from the outside. These holy objects, just as they helped us with the litany-meditation, can help us remember that our guardian angel is standing at our shoulder and that we can rely on him.

I will say it once again: these objects have no magic power in themselves, but we can, without any superstition, invest them with the power to connect with divine energy. We could say that they serve as catalysts for the support of the Gods. We can, for example, take a wooden statuette, a crucifix, an image of the Virgin Mary, a stone, a crystal or an amethyst, and magnetize it by touching it with our hands. We transmit our own vibrations to the object, by saying, 'Protect me. If anybody wishes me any harm, be my shield. Negative thoughts will not reach me, because you are going to intercept them.' But be careful! Your talisman must serve only to repel negative thoughts. It must not do anyone harm. When magnetizing it, we should see to it that our prayer is pure, devoid of any negative intentions, and that we do not endow it with any malicious power over others.

When we have terrible doubts, perhaps regarding a trip we are about to make or some other project, a blessed medal of the Virgin can be an excellent support. Obviously we can't go around carrying a statue of Buddha or a Russian icon, but we can be reassured by a small object which we can take with us in our pocket and so always have to hand. As matter of fact, we are protected by numerous entities, but for us they are perhaps not tangible enough. So we endow these objects with the power to represent that protection, to remind us of the benevolence of our guardian angel, of that being of light who is always with us. The Bible tells us how the Hebrews used to wear phylacteries (literally 'that which protects') on the left arm or the forehead – small leather pouches in which slips of parchment or vellum were enclosed, containing passages from the Law of Moses.

At first I practised these protection techniques, but as I progressed I was able to discard them. They become useless once the initiate reaches the second stage, which we will deal with later. At that point one realizes that love protects one far more efficiently than any talisman.

It may also happen that we come upon places charged with negative vibrations, which are not expressly directed towards us, but nevertheless, we may suffer their harmful influence. Some houses, for example, may have witnessed terrible events or been the home of people with bad intentions, and consequently the walls are still charged with accumulated negativity. It can also happen that a house is badly situated, which puts it in conflict with the web of telluric forces.

But, it is important to point out that such houses are very rare. And we should not assume that our apartment has been taken over by evil forces because three bulbs blew on the same evening! Before calling an exorcist, consult your electrician! To believe that we are being persecuted by demonic forces all the time is yet another deviation created by the mind, to distract us from our real responsibilities.

However, it is possible to come across such a house and there might be a real need to neutralize its malevolent energies, or we may simply want to purify a house we are moving into. There are 'magical' practices to be performed in these cases. This is 'white' magic, and not 'black' magic. The former is that which is done on behalf of and with the help of celestial forces for the benefit of man. It is the application of those faculties which we originally possessed, while we still enjoyed our divine nature. The royal art of alchemy is none other than an attempt gradually to return to that pure nature. Black magic is the opposite; it has negative, criminal intentions.

The only permissible magic is that which is prompted by a disinterested desire to help. The Cabbalah does not speak of magic, but prefers the word *theurgy*, which is the art of producing effects in the divine sphere, with a redemptive aim and not for selfish ends. It is about attaining knowledge about man and nature in order to act favourably on both. Theurgy is therefore the art of assuring the passage between these two energy levels. Thanks to certain practices, we have the means to reach out and touch those invisible realms: 'what is below awakens what is above,' said a formula of the *Zohar*, the Book of Splendour of the Cabbalists. Everything can influence everything and people here below can establish contact with higher worlds.

Sometimes, I resort to certain traditional practices I inherited from my family. When moving to a new house or apartment, for example, and being aware of negative vibrations, I would put a large handful of sea salt on a white dish or on a white sheet of paper in each of the four corners of the house or apartment. I insist on sea salt because it has been obtained by evaporation, and so is, according to Louis-Claude de Saint-Martin 'the fire delivered from the waters', which makes it a great purifier. When putting down the salt, it is important to ask it to swallow all the negative energies which linger around the house. The following day, go back and throw the salt out of the house: it will then be entirely purified. As far as energies are concerned, the house has become neutral; you have just carried out a total cleansing. It is up to you now to impregnate that place with your presence and to make of it what you will.

Most religions recognize the protective value of salt. The Muslims know it well. Asians use it as a matter of course to purify places which they consider to have been soiled; they sprinkle salt on the threshold of their houses to protect them from harmful influences. In the same way the Sumo wrestler throws salt on the circle where the combat is to occur, so that it may take place in a spirit of loyalty.

By the same token, after the departure of a malicious person who has come to bother you in your home and whose bad intentions you want to clear away, throw a handful of salt on to the doorstep, then sweep it towards the outside of the house: that person will not come back to bother you. I insist once again, however, that we must do all this without any negative intentions regarding the intruder, but simply as a preventative measure.

It's nevertheless possible that certain presences may resist the action of sea salt. The soul of a dead person who passed away in a particular place may continue to inhabit that space. At the moment of death it refused to leave this world and clung on to matter, and now haunts the walls, the furniture and other objects. That departed being is asking to be remembered. There is no reason to be afraid of those 'ghosts'; they mean us no harm. They have simply realized that remaining eternal prisoners on earth is a terrible plight and they are asking us for help by demonstrating their presence, by making the wood of the furniture crack violently, by moving objects, by creating strange phenomena. In such a case the situation is reversed; it's not you who needs help, but you who can give the help.

Put four beeswax candles, if possible blessed by being sprinkled with holy water, with prayers to support that blessing, around the object which you consider 'possessed'. If it's a room, place those candles in the four corners. At the moment of lighting the wicks, you must say a prayer, asking that the flame which rises up may help bring you protection and positive energy. This is a valid rule for every time you light a candle or a stick of incense, for example, during your meditation exercises. Never light a candle or incense stick without praying and asking for blessings, otherwise negative forces might profit from it. That could be more dangerous than doing nothing. The Orientals tell us that we must pray before lighting incense. You need only say 'May this stick of incense protect me.' Then the smoke of the incense will increase its protective powers. If you don't take these precautions, you run the risk of intensifying negative energies.

Once the candles are lit around the object, let them burn. You have just created an upward-moving circle of energy. The soul which was anchored in matter will find itself projected into the astral world, released from the furniture or the walls. The Cosmos will be grateful to you for performing this ritual, because you will have helped a soul locked on this intermediary level and helped its ascension towards divinity. You will have performed an act of mercy.

In the same spirit, with the same desire to liberate souls held captive in matter, whenever I enter a church I light a candle for a lost soul. I say the following prayer: 'May the first wandering soul passing over this site use the light of this candle as an exit to go from the intermediary level towards the light of divinity.' I whisper these words aloud or say them to myself. At that moment, if often happens that the flame of my candle doubles or triples in size, and then I know that one of the dead held prisoner on this plane has found its way to salvation.

On this subject, I would like to remind you that it is wise to pray for our dead, but not to invoke their help. When a soul leaves this earth, it begins a journey during which it has to rise in search of God, while accepting that it may have to return to this world to resolve its karma. If we appeal to the dead for help, the soul will turn towards the earth, towards this lowly plane, instead of continuing on its ascensional journey. The dead have other concerns than to come to our rescue. For this purpose, we have at our disposal a multitude of enlightened entities: the Principalities, the Thrones, the Powers, the Dominations; the Cherubim, the Seraphim, the Archangels, the Angels and the Saints. They are all part of that divine kingdom and it's them we have to hassle, if you'll forgive the familiarity! Ask them to act on your behalf, and they will.

But not just in any old way. If you have decided that St Anthony is the saint to invoke over lost objects, while not being wrong, it shows a certain naiveté on your part. There is so much more to be gained from St Anthony, St Teresa, St Expeditus, the Archangel Gabriel, St Michael and so many others: your guardian angel, the great patriarchs . . . All these celestial hierarchies are at your disposal; ask them to intercede with God in your favour, to find your keys or get you a job, if that's what you want, but you would also do well to ask them to 'show you the way', both in your everyday life and in your spiritual life.

To light a candle at the foot of a statue helps your request rise towards them. Nevertheless, a precaution must be taken: light your candle with a match or a lighter, or with the flames of three other candles. For if you light your candle with just one other flame from another votive candle, you are perpetuating the wish of the person who put it there and you might be running the risk of contributing to a malevolent act. Some devotees ask God some very weird things . . . Don't become their accomplice. Use the first flame, then a second, then a third: that little 'magic trick' will eliminate the negative intentions which might have been linked to one or other of these flames. Your personal wish will then ascend freely to the saint you invoked or towards any other higher being.

And before asking to be spared hindrances, illnesses, betrayals and dangers of all kinds, start by asking that your inner demons be overcome . . .

When we think of adversity, we tend to think of it as being external, as something that happens to us. But, in fact, what does happen to us? Events that we cannot escape, that we are going to have to overcome or avoid which had resulted simply from our misguided behaviour. In such a case, there is only one thing to do: change that behaviour. We should try to be true to ourselves and become more conscious of our actions. That is precisely what one looks for when starting psychotherapy.

Having said that, many psychologists will tell you that to add a sacred dimension to that intellectual clearing can only improve the results of psychological treatment. Since Adam's fall, the forces of evil have insinuated themselves into our psyches and surreptitiously exerted their negative influence. These forces are all the negative passions – pride, envy, hatred – which we nurture inside us, every one of us, if we are honest enough to admit it. Most of us have one of two attitudes towards our dark side. Some work at repressing it, burying it deep inside themselves. This is a short-term measure, for these demons then slowly eat us up from within, fashioning our behaviour from our unconscious, and every day we grow further away from our own truth. Besides, these walls are fragile: the day will come when these repressed feelings will re-emerge, stronger than ever . . .

To try to stop this inner corrosion, the other attitude is to give free expression to those demons, to externalize them each time they manifest: we blow up in rage, we no longer hide our envy, we flaunt our pride . . . and we waste our lives.

We should avoid both these approaches and have the courage to confront those inner dragons. We should kill that part of us which is driven by passion, by that 'libido' which Freud describes as being so much more than sexual, governing almost all of our behaviour. Let's try to vanquish the eternal enemy, the winged dragon that St Michael and St George confronted with their spears. On the central porch of Notre-Dame in Paris, there is a statue of a crowned adept holding the book of Wisdom, crushing with his spear the dragon being born from an alchemist who sleeps in his bed. The same symbolism is found in the image of the Virgin's delicate foot crushing the ancient serpent, thus giving back to the initiate the virginity of his spirit. The reference is to the initiatory death of the old man, followed by the rebirth of the new man, virgin and pure.

But for man to die of his old foolish ways and for the young man to be reborn pure, the work is colossal. It involves delving into our darkest regions, tracking down the perversions of our will. It does not mean being contrite and self-indulgently beating our breast while thinking 'I am a miserable sinner'. Self-blame is sometimes too comfortable. We become resigned to our faults, saying, 'That's how I am, what a shame, but there is nothing I can do about it.' No, what is needed, first of all, is that we don't lie to ourselves, that we learn to know who we are without being complacent and with the firm intention of improving. The Sufis compare the soul to an oxidized mirror with rust covering its surface. 'Whoever wants to restore it, will have two chores to perform,' Ghazali, the eleventh-century Muslim philosopher tells us, 'rub and polish . . . If, giving in to his appetites, man persists in provoking the causes which bring about the accumulation of rust on the mirror of his soul, his aptitude to reflect the truth will be totally eclipsed.'

The problem is that the old man in us does not go away that easily! We know that he poisons our life, but we end up by growing attached to him, we even think to ourselves that the place will seem very empty once he's gone. Nevertheless, we need to overcome the winged dragon of our lively imagination. We have calmed the mind, paid attention to our daily habits; the moment has arrived for deeper purification. And we might as well know that it will take great effort. Remember the labours of Hercules! When King Augeas asked Hercules to clean his stables, the task seemed impossible. What did Hercules do? He dug a trench and diverted the course of a river. The current of water swept away all the horse dung. What is this story about, apart from being a tale about a stableman? This myth shows that learning receptivity and opening one's heart will help us understand that big problems require extreme solutions; that drastic measures will have to be taken to dispose of what remains of all the trappings of matter, of all the unacknowledged and unexpressed wishes, all the unhealthy disturbances, all the complex desires, all the dreams of domination and power. A superficial clearing away is not enough; we need to purify ourselves thoroughly, without cheating.

Now the time has come for our descent into the inferno of the alchemists, the Black Opus symbolized by the crow repeatedly hitting the ground with his beak, to make the worms believe that raindrops are falling on the earth. Then the worms come to the surface and the crow eats them: the rot of the earth is thus eradicated.

As for that Black Opus, only you can do it; nobody here on earth can help you. There is no need to go into a retreat to accomplish this Work. No doubt it would help you to take stock of the situation, to create the necessary distance, but the battle must be fought every single day.

To fire your enthusiasm, you must know that not only will your karma benefit from this hard task, but your earthly happiness will also be enhanced.

To prepare for introspection, there is a simple exercise which should be practised every day: examine your conscience. Once again, it's no use repeating, 'It's my own fault,' and then inflicting on yourself a penance for your so-called 'sins', only to repeat them the next day. It is imperative to proceed with total honesty when examining the conscience. After all, even seminars bringing together the executives of large companies advise them to take stock of the situation regarding human resource problems. Did I behave properly with so and so? Was I wrong to lose my temper? Have I lied unashamedly under the pretext of being diplomatic, when in reality I was being cowardly? All these questions aim at changing people's behaviour, at improving management and professional life within a company.

Examining our conscience goes further than this, obviously. It delves much deeper and the aim is not just greater spiritual harmony, but also to find happiness again on our earthly path.

Again I need to stress that the quest for enlightenment is not about frustration and renunciation; it is a liberation which will benefit our lives, including our daily existence.

If we think about it, what is it that most makes our lives seem fake? Greed, envy, anger, sloth – or is it mainly pride? It certainly is pride, the capital sin. Most of our faults are caused by pride.

Pride makes us compare our lot with that of others, so much so that we end up by trying to mix with those whose success we envy, despite not always admiring them. We need to forget about the social whirl, but at the same time we must not think we are superior to others either; that would be the worst kind of pride.

Pride makes us cultivate power for power's sake, whereas the only true way to exercise power is to assume responsibility. The rest is but deviation: vanity, frantic greed for ostentatious pleasures, embarking on love affairs with people just because they are rich or famous, sexual promiscuity, debauchery and the cruelty which follows when we realize that none of these things are able to satisfy us.

Pride generates a need to be constantly recognized and loved. A very human frailty, no doubt, but one which often makes us betray ourselves and others just to give us pleasure. A desire for recognition beyond what our immediate circle can offer provokes in us tremendous rages and self-centred anger – that is when it does not become a persecution complex. Whereas if we weren't quite so lazy, we would first of all try to love ourselves, accept ourselves as we are, and then try to improve. We would then be far less desperate for declarations of love and compliments, and ironically, that's when we would receive them.

Pride is thus the ultimate temptation – thinking of ourselves as future saints! We should be content to be initiates, people who have started on the path, and not people who know everything. We should beware of false revelations. I understand that people have a need for spiritual experiences in these materialistic times, but we need to be careful where we go looking for them. Be wary of those who claim to have discovered hidden knowledge, for the true inner path is built on humility.

To tame that satanic pride, which was the primary cause of Adam's fall, there is nothing like examining our conscience. The Sufis put great emphasis on this and considered it one of the best means of approaching perfection. Some masters recommend that we should write down in a notebook, morning and night, all the thoughts, intentions, acts and words which could have led us to stray from the path. 'Ask your soul to account for its thoughts and actions, before Allah does,' the Prophet tells us.

Here again, we should ask for God's help, but in a different way. Knowing that even if we have to endure trials for which we don't understand the reason, we are nevertheless responsible for our own problems. We need to chase away our own inner demons, knowing that they won't depart easily. Our vices have deep roots; it's not enough just to decide rationally to eliminate them.

The harshness of this fight with Satan, who has insinuated himself into our psyche – for that is what we are dealing with here – is powerfully expressed in the Bible's Psalms, as well as in the Koran, and also in Buddhism, where the faithful clamour for the destruction of their enemies: 'Brandish the spear and the spike against my persecutors!', 'Break the teeth in their mouths' and 'Make those imposters perish . . .'. Those imposters, those infidels who persecute the just, are not so much physical people, but our inner demons. For Islam, the famous Holy War, the *jihad*, unfortunately often interpreted as military conquest, is no other than the 'effort on the path to God'. This is so true that the Sufis, to emphasize the difference, call the armed combat fought by hand, the 'little jihad' and the battle which a man must wage against his passions the 'big jihad'.

We have to be like warriors, ever ready for battle. Buddha, whose pacifism is well-known, is sometimes depicted as a soldier clad in armour. The victory we hope for is the one we will celebrate once the ego is vanquished, once the anarchy of demonic powers is overcome. It will mean the victory of those living forces which govern our inner equilibrium, the realization of oneness, the discovery of our innermost core and the restoration of the Light.

When we are thus restructured, our relationships with others should improve greatly. We must remember that the nature of our feelings is conveyed to those around us by waves of energy. If we are in harmony with ourselves, people will feel 'well' when they are near and not wish us any harm.

The expression 'hell is other people' is a devilish trap. It re-inforces our self-indulgence, persuading us that our failures, whether in love or work, are not our responsibility. It is, above all, a real manifestation of pride: are we so important that the whole of humanity should want to ally itself against us?

Having said that, it is also true that others don't always harbour good intentions towards us. Some people reveal themselves to be actually malevolent and their thoughts, full of hatred, can affect and weaken us, making our actions useless.

Nevertheless, there is no need to think you are possessed by evil spirits every time you feel tormented by inexplicable forces. Real cases of possession are very rare. But, it is true that even the Church recognizes their existence, because it has priests who are exorcists and who can easily be contacted through the Catholic hierarchy. In some animistic cultures, such as those in Africa, one can find people who are capable of capturing someone's thoughts and thereby taking away their free will, by means of magnetic and vibrational energies. As a general rule, our enemies don't go to those lengths to harm us. The cousin we are fighting with over an inheritance, or the office colleague who would like to have your job, won't necessarily spend the weekend pushing needles through a wax effigy made in your image. What such people can do is send us negative vibrations and wish so desperately for things to go wrong for us, that they manage to disturb us without our knowledge, interfering with our concentration and undermining our self-confidence.

The more honest will show their dislike openly, attacking our work or our family. Others go about it in an underhand manner, disguising their hatred with deceitful smiles, secretly mulling over their dark plans. Without developing a persecution mania every time things don't work out as planned, we can be alerted by encountering repeated and inexplicable pitfalls, an abnormal feeling of exhaustion, negative thoughts which come to us suddenly, unexpected bouts of laziness, unusual rages, resentments or feelings of discouragement. When these feelings are particularly strong, there is one unmistakable sign that these vibrations are occurring – we no longer feel like praying any more, we forget to do it, or we cannot do it.

That is precisely the moment to make the effort to read the sacred texts, reading every line, every word, out loud and without faltering. The Bible's Psalms in no way deny the reality of these assaults from our external enemies: 'Be gracious to me, O God, for men trample upon me; all day foemen oppress me,' we read in Psalm 56. 'Deliver me from my enemies, my God, protect me from my aggressors, deliver me from the wicked ones, from men of blood, save me.' Jesus himself, when he is setting free a child who is possessed, a 'demonic epileptic', says to his disciples, *'This kind cannot be driven out by anything but prayer.'* (Mark 9: 28.)

Apart from asking for divine protection, we can also use practical techniques for protection without letting ourselves be drawn into a power struggle. It is not a question of returning blow for blow, but of neutralizing an attack without any resentment.

We have already mentioned the use of sea salt for the protection of houses against undesirable spirits. One could also use water which has great purifying qualities. When you meet someone whom you feel has a strong negative aura, go into the bathroom and splash generous amounts of water on your arms, around the elbow joint. All negative energies will thus be intercepted and washed away with the water as it flows over the elbows. It's an efficient form of protection to use every time you have mentioned someone who makes you feel ill-at-ease or when you have shaken hands with someone potentially harmful – the demands of professional life are such that we can hardly avoid this kind of contact. Let's not forget the power of holy water, with which you can sprinkle either your house or your place of work, without necessarily thinking about a specific person, but just to disarm unknown enemies.

One of my favourite protection techniques is the use of a mirror. The Taoists endow it with the virtue of revealing the nature of harmful influences and repelling them. They often place a small mirror above their door for this purpose. Similarly the shamans of Asia have fragments of mirrors sewn onto their clothes, meant to protect them from the darts of mischievous spirits. Perhaps I subconsciously made use of this principle when I created dresses made of small plaques of polished metal which reflected back images like mirrors . . .

However, there are several mirror techniques, or rather variants of the same technique. We have already mentioned the 'egg of light', which can shield you in public places. Now, suppose that someone practises black magic against you, or simply attacks you with negative vibrations. As a precaution, when you're at home meditate and visualize yourself as a mirror. Then imagine the person in question as a dark silhouette in front of you and address them thus: 'See yourself in this mirror; everything you send me in love, I give you back a thousandfold.' If that person has only positive feelings for you, they will be rewarded by extraordinary blessings. On the other hand, if they have had negative thoughts, the rebound will be terrible and automatic . . . It won't be you who formulated the wish, since you only alluded to what was sent 'with love'. This is actually a cosmic law and I would recommend that you remember it whenever you catch yourself wishing someone harm, for there's a good chance those thoughts will come rebounding back on you sooner or later.

Another technique involves containing the person who may have bad intentions towards you. It may be someone who is secretly scheming, or someone who is treating you unfairly, someone who is envious of you, a colleague who is plotting your downfall, a boss who exploits you, or a woman driven by jealousy. Visualize your persecutors as if they were inside a cube covered with mirrors. Wherever they turn, they will find themselves confronted with their own bad thoughts and actions. Not only will their negative vibrations be neutralized at source, but you will be giving them the opportunity to become conscious of their evildoing. 'How can one take revenge on one's enemies?' someone asked Diogenes. 'By making an honest man out of him,' he replied without hesitation.

But, there again, you must remember not to spoil this technique by combining it with your own animosity. 'A soft answer turns away wrath, but a harsh word stirs up anger,' we read in Proverbs 15: 1. 'Treat well whoever seeks to quarrel with you, and to whoever does you harm, give him love in return,' says a Babylonian proverb. We should, therefore, surround that cage of mirrors with absolute love, asking God to help the person inside. Don't be afraid that he or she might use that help to hurt you. The celestial powers will never lend their support to evil intentions.

Be vigilant regarding what motivates your protection exercises! I am sometimes horrified to hear certain false guides advise their disciples to visualize burying their enemies in concrete! A criminal thought like that will only weigh down your karma.

And you will lose the benevolent protection of your guardian angel. For the celestial powers will only protect us for as long as we are just. If, during your meditation, you ask for a selfish favour that will bring harm to others, the divine entities will not help; quite the contrary. Receiving a shock instead will wake us up and open our eyes . . . This is more common than one imagines; people do use their medals or other talismans to do evil deeds, then they are astonished when, sooner or later, they reap the consequences of their harmful thoughts. If you are tempted to do so, remember Psalm 7: 12–17:

> If a man does not repent, God will whet his sword; he has bent and strung his bow; he has prepared his deadly weapons, making his arrows fiery shafts. Behold, the wicked man conceives evil, and is pregnant with mischief; and brings forth lies. He makes a pit, digging it out, and falls into the hole which he has made. His mischief returns upon his own head, and on his own pate his violence descends.

That warning is all the more important in my view in that the initiate will, no doubt, be faced on his quest with the temptation to exercise over others the powers he discovers. For the more we approach self-knowledge, the more our ability to act on the psychic plane develops. This new situation has its own perils. I recounted in my book *Journey* how in my youth I used my gifts as a medium to further my own personal interests and how I paid a high price for doing so. Esoteric research is not necessarily plain sailing; it can be a path littered with dangerous risks. If misunderstood and applied in the wrong way, the quest becomes destructive. Some will seek out the 'sacred fire' of knowledge only to use it for their own purposes, whereas we should enter this world of symbols with a pure, clear spirit, with the intention of helping others and expanding our own consciousness.

Furthermore, if the initiate is humble and sincere, he will realize that the best protection, as far as other people are concerned, is the positive thought he radiates towards them. That positive field is our strongest shield, for it stops our enemies from harming us. It may at first seem strange, but it is in wishing them the very best that we are safeguarded. And you will find that the person in question will forget you, or even better, become conscious of the destructive effects of their behaviour and will approach you for reconciliation. For you, the rewards will be doubled; you will have put a stop to their hostility and your positive thoughts will have been returned to you as positive energy. For no one escapes, either for good or evil, the law of the 'boomerang' effect.

I can hear you protest: 'It's not that easy to wish someone well when that person is out to harm you deliberately. And how can I wish my rival the happiness he covets, when that would mean taking my place, in someone's heart or at the office?'

You will be spared these difficulties if, instead of cursing your persecutors, you pray for them. For there again, their happiness is not what they are thinking of, but what God has in store for them. And it is so much easier to pray for someone who has harmed us than consciously to wish them well. By doing that we leave behind our petty reasoning, which only takes into consideration our material self, and act according to the higher teachings given by Christ:

> You have heard that it was said, 'You shall love your neighbour and hate your enemy.' Well, I say to you, Love your enemies and pray for those who persecute you, so that you may be the sons of your Father who is in heaven; for he makes the sun rise on the evil and on the good, and sends rain on the just and the unjust. (Matthew 5: 43–45)

Clearly, the bestowing of both punishments and rewards is God's prerogative. Regarding others, we should try to smooth out everyday quarrels and jealousies and take a step forward, towards an understanding which seems so scarce in these final years of the Age of Steel. As Monsignor Gaillot[11] said: 'Once one has prayed for people, one cannot see them in the same light . . .'

It is time to remember that we are all divine creatures and, seeing the immense danger with which we are threatened in these years of violence, we would do well to unite, instead of attacking each other. Let's put our petty quarrels aside; they are but dust as far as the Cosmos is concerned. We should seek to re-establish a relationship with creation, and we will feel much more serene as a result.

5

Finding One's Place in the Cosmos

*All things are in harmony with me, who am in harmony
with thee, oh universe. Nothing is too precocious or too late,
of what is seasonable to thee. All things are fruit for me,
which your seasons bring, oh nature: for everything comes
from thee, everything is within thee and returns to thee.*
MARCUS AURELIUS ANTONIUS (Roman Emperor 151–80 CE)

'God, creator of Heaven and Earth.' When we think of how much
natural beauty there is on earth, when we imagine the thousands
of stars, planets and galaxies which make up the Cosmos, we are
filled with wonder and a sense of religious awe. It is a pity that
everybody could not share the astronauts' experience, the extraordinary opportunity to take in the whole of Gaia's great luminous
sphere in one glance, to have an overview of the blue planet. Such
a global vision would give us a glimpse of cosmic wholeness and
show us the powerful convergence between the Universe and our
own selves. One can easily imagine that such a vision might well
change a person's behaviour. For, paradoxically, far from feeling
insignificant faced with that vastness, one would discover that one
is part of that cosmic whole, of creation, and so every one of us,
thank God, is of enormous importance.

Nevertheless we do need to establish ourselves in relation to the

Cosmos, truly feeling that we share its essence and experience its joy.

Alas, we are not all astronauts. The end of the Piscean Age seems to be characterized by people who live in places they don't like and their 'dis-ease' seems to be due in great part to the disharmony they feel with regard their environment. This is especially true if they live in an urban area, which is the case for the majority of the population in the so-called developed countries.

To live in the present means concentrating on the here and now. We are evolving in space and in time, and the two cannot be dissociated. Unfortunately, we make the same mistake regarding both space and time. We hanker after living a simple life or we dream of an exotic 'elsewhere'. We forget that we chose the place where we live at the moment of our incarnation on earth. Before actually reincarnating here, we chose our parents, and by the same token, chose a place, a particular tradition and culture. This can seem terrible to someone with unkind parents or born into dire poverty. Nevertheless, these are the tools we chose to accomplish the task of lightening our karma. So why do we feel so uprooted, stateless or simple unbalanced?

I often meet people who are dissatisfied with their circumstances and with the place they live in. They always say the same thing: 'I would love to leave this town, this apartment, these surroundings!' I reply invariably, 'If you're uncomfortable here, that means you're at odds with yourself. You'll be the same person, even if you go somewhere else. Moving will not solve the problem.'

Wherever we go, we always have to take ourselves along with us. So, before we start thinking of packing, instead of changing the scenery, why not try to change our relationship with the world?

We will have taken a great step forward, the day we admit that our happiness has to be found where we are, by reconciling ourselves with our own dwelling place, which is what we have been trying to do from the beginning of our quest. That abode, as we have seen, is our body and our soul, but it is also the physical space in which we evolve and which we can extend in ever-growing

100

concentric circles – a room, a town, a planet, the whole Cosmos . . .
But we should never forget that everything emerges from the
centre of our being. And the only voyage that matters is the one
which the Knights of the Round Table undertook in their quest for
the Holy Grail. When they came back empty-handed to King
Arthur's court at Camelot, Merlin welcomed them with the
following question: 'Have you found what you were looking for?'
Crestfallen, they admitted their failure. The magician laughingly
told them, 'Sit at the Round Table and go on your journey again,
but this time take a voyage within yourselves.' That Round Table
symbolizes both the centre of our being, as well as the circle of
cosmic infinity. We are reminded of Buddha's words: 'The best
movement is in stillness, for it is thus that we find the Universe
in ourselves.'

We will find that by meditating we can attain this internal
revelation of the Universe, but to do so we have to be further along
the path. Meanwhile, knowing that these riches are there for us,
offered by this world-cathedral, we should take advantage of
them, instead of considering our environment hostile or enslaving
it at our whim. We must remember that it is only when we are
ensnared by the material and possessed by inertia that matter
becomes satanic: Nature in itself is magnificent, full of the
splendours God created! We should begin, therefore, by humbly
recontacting the magic of our planet, its divine beauty, and the
spirits which dwell on it and which are far from being hostile. We
must rediscover the enchantment of earthly reality and use the
elements to regenerate ourselves. Once we have done this, realizing the treasures which we still have at our disposal, we may
feel committed to preserving them.

One could argue that it is difficult to conceive of the splendours of
the earth when we live subjected to urban aggression, such as
constant noise, concrete buildings, pollution and traffic jams. And
yet, a few kilometres away from the great urban centres, there
are still prairies, forests, rivers, marshes, lakes, waterfalls, country

lanes. Why is it that apart from those days when people go picking mushrooms or gathering wild flowers, these place are always empty? Modern man has a tendency to view nature as an irrational force which it is his mission to tame, by building dams to control the large rivers, investing in motorways or high speed trains, exhausting the soil – that is, when he does not just transform it into a vast dustbin. Subsequently, without the slightest shame, he declares that environment hostile, disfigured, 'not like in the old days', thinking only of the corruption of his surroundings instead of looking around and discovering, nearby, what remains that is divine. We think of road-building as progress, we talk about our location, as if to unconsciously underline the fact that we are contained, imprisoned in it, hesitating between a lethargic cocooning and a disagreeable claustrophobia. We feel cornered, suffocating, without air . . .

We need to change our outlook and get closer to everything on earth that pulsates with life and vibrates with energy. For all around us, in an incessant ballet, the four elements, water, air, fire and earth, the basis of esoteric and sacred tradition, mingle. There are so many vital powers which we need to rediscover and learn how to use again.

At the dawn of the Age of Aquarius, we should put ourselves in tune with those simple elements of which nature is made up. Our daily well-being, as well as humanity's survival, is dependent on being able to incorporate that sweet animism. We should go back to harmonizing rituals, imitating whenever we can the alchemist who, before performing his experiments, never failed to recite Hermes Trismegistus' ancient hymn: 'Universe, be attentive to my prayer! Earth, open yourself, so that the mass of waters may open to me. Trees, do not tremble: I want to pay homage to the Lord of Creation, the Whole and the One. May the heavens open and the winds grow silent. May all the faculties within me celebrate the Whole and the One.'

I have already mentioned the purifying and reviving qualities of the first element, which is water. Both doctors and holiday-makers know the therapeutic value of both sea-bathing and hot springs. But if we view this bathing as a sacred ritual, we will be all the more energized. Simply contemplating the sea can be as beneficial as bathing in it and as helpful as drinking mineral water. The Tao attributes incomparable teaching properties to water:

Transcendent goodness is like water,

Water likes to benefit all beings;

It does not struggle for any shape or definite position

But occupies the lowly places no one wants.

By doing that, it is the image of Principle.

Following its example, those who lower themselves, who dig into themselves,

Are benevolent, sincere, ordered, effective and adapted to the times.

The second element is fire. The sun is our natural source of fire. Meditation in the light of the morning sun is certainly one of the best ways of restoring our energies. With eyes half closed, in a contemplative position, we suddenly feel penetrated and filled by luminous rays which 'recharge our batteries' almost instantly, as if the body was a solar panel. The efficiency of your meditation technique can thus be multiplied.

But, be careful, for the elements can be either beneficial or harmful. To expose yourself to the afternoon sun, like all those people who go to the beach at two in the afternoon, is dangerous. The white or blue light of the morning is calm and healing, but the red or orange sun at its zenith destroys, causes skin burns and even skin cancer.

The earth which sustains us is itself a marvellous provider of energy. That is why, according to Hindu tradition, the first task for the meditator is to anchor himself to the earth, finding a stable sitting position, so as to help the flow of energy between the heavens and Gaia. To sit on the ground or to walk on grass are beneficial acts, provided we don't make a superstition of them.

They are ways of getting in touch with creation, of contacting divine will.

Crystals and stones are an intrinsic part of the earth and nowadays we are rediscovering the power that was attributed to them by ancient tradition, thousands of years ago. That power has nothing to do with their market value. You can buy crystals which cost very little and yet obtain great benefits from them. You can also buy uncut precious or semi-precious stones, which greatly reduces their cost.

Amber, for example, is not expensive and is quite easy to find nowadays. The Greeks and Romans used to travel thousands of miles to the Baltic countries to obtain it. It is a resin, up to seven million years old, which comes from ancient coniferous trees. That link between its mineral and vegetable aspects gives amber great healing and protective powers. I have an amber stone which was quite dull at first, but I awoke it by stroking it and today it shines with an astonishing brilliance.

The subjects of crystals and gemstones is vast, and there are many books written on the virtues of stones and crystals, amethysts, quartz, onyx, turquoises, sapphires, tourmalines, and so on. It is up to the reader to make his own selection. I would just like to draw your attention to the fact that one should not handle stones carelessly, without knowing their particular qualities and their power. These vary greatly, according to how they were formed. Some crystals grow towards the right, others towards the left. The first accelerate and amplify energy and can, therefore, be used to revitalize us, but they can also, occasionally, prove dangerous. If you are ill, they will reactivate the pathological process.

The stones with formations to the left will, on the contrary, 'swallow' energies. If you hold them in your hand when meditating, or rub them on a diseased part of your body, they can absorb negative energies and malignant growths; but on the other hand, they may weaken you, for they will equally absorb positive energies.

I gave one of my friends an amethyst. Before going to sleep, she puts the amethyst in the middle of her forehead, on the brow chakra, to get rid of the stress accumulated during the day. She tells me that the result is spectacular. Nevertheless, I advised her not to leave the amethyst beside her all night and to take trace element supplements to replace any energy lost through her nightly practice.

How can you tell if you're dealing with an energizing or 'liberating' stone? If you are sensitive to such energies, you can feel it instinctively. You can also observe its effects (whether it aggravates or gets rid of headaches, stress or other ailments) to know if your stone's formation is oriented to the left or to the right.

I don't have to point out that the benefits of gemstones and crystals cannot replace medical advice, in the event of health problems occurring! Rocks have neither miraculous powers nor diagnostic capacities – they don't go to medical school!

As for air, whether at the seaside, in the mountains or in the countryside, common sense has always told us of its virtues. However, fresh air has now become a rare commodity and we are now changing our tune. The air in our towns has become impure. Globally, the atmosphere has become ever more polluted, and, consequently, harmful to our health. The foulness of the air we breathe is certainly somewhat to blame for the widespread violence which we see everywhere in the world today. Studies have shown that black clouds of pollution hover above our cities and have a direct influence on our levels of aggression and stress. How can we free ourselves from this heavy stench?

Whatever happens, we should try as often as possible to find somewhere to breathe in the air free from car pollution. Symbolically, air represents the subtle world, which links heaven and earth. In the Bible it was considered as a vehicle of knowledge and messages. David consulted God by listening to the rustling of the wind in the crown of balsam trees (II Samuel 5: 24). When we practise breathing exercises, while preparing for meditation, let's remember that breath is synonymous with the divine spirit, the breath of life transmitted by God to man. We should learn once more to listen for that voice in both the light breeze and in the squalls of the tempest.

Anyone who has never felt wonder listening to the rustling of leaves in the wind or the murmur of a brook, crumbled earth through his fingers or thrilled to the pulsating energies of a stone, it to be pitied; he is one of those people who, although they have eyes to see and ears to hear, don't see or hear anything at all!

When we learn to make use of all that is offered to us daily, we will store up amazing treasures of strength and joy. The man who follows that path will be 'like a tree planted by running streams, that yields its fruit in its season, and its leaf does not wither. In all that he does, he prospers.' (Psalm 1: 3.)

When I contemplate Nature, I pay particular attention to trees, perhaps because they combine the four elements so bountifully – their roots in the earth, the water which mingles with their sap, the fire hidden in their wood, ready to emerge, and finally the air which shakes their leaves and is purified in the process.

How can we fail to feel reverence and humility before these giants, which date back so many centuries – sometimes even millennia, as with the *Sequoia gigantea* – and breathe strength and vibrate with life force? Rising towards heaven, they are symbols of the spiritual growth of the Cosmos. All civilizations have worshipped trees: the Celtic oak, renowned for its strength and longevity; the birch, sacred tree of the Siberian people; the olive tree which is the symbol of peace; the cedar of Lebanon, which is said to be the oldest tree in the world, and now threatened with extinction . . . How can one wander into a forest, among those 'living pillars', and not feel as though in nature's cathedral?

When I go for a walk among clusters of trees, I love to feel their rough bark, thanking them for the oxygen they give us. On evenings when the moon is rising, to lean one's back against a tree trunk is to feel tremendously energized. In certain Indian traditions, as well as in Africa and North America, the bride and groom had literally to kiss the trees to protect their union from evil spirits and to assure their fertility.

In all religions, the tree is a symbol of life and knowledge. It was under a Bodhi tree, on the banks of the Phalgu river, that prince Gautama was 'awakened' and became the Buddha. In the Koran it describes how it was under the 'jujube tree of Al Montaha' that the Prophet of Islam had a vision of an angel (Sura 53: 14). At the centre of the garden of Eden grew the Tree of Life, that *axis mundi* around which the Cosmos is organized. 'Every sacred site in the world is placed at the foot of a sacred tree,' says the *Shiva Purana*, before listing a series of instructions for reaping the benefits of these:

> Whoever adores the Great God under the guise of a lingam at the foot of the Bilva tree, will have his soul purified and attain Shiva . . . The one who pours water on his head at the base of a sacred tree can consider that he has bathed in all the sacred waters of the earth. In truth, he is sanctified . . . The man who accomplishes the adoration ritual by offering perfumes and flowers at the foot of a Bilva tree enters the sphere of Shiva. His happiness increases, his family prospers.

Far from prospering, the human race is destroying itself; we are destroying all our forests, in particular the rainforests, which constitute (or once constituted?) our safety belt, a huge reserve of plant and animal species . . . Deprived of this cosmic pillar, the earth runs the risk of floundering into chaos again . . .

But be reassured, I am not suggesting that we go back to living in trees! It's not a question of calling for a return to Nature in the strictest sense, but for an awakening and the realization that Nature is our lifeline. We cannot live without it.

Clearly, we need to be able to feel this sense of the sacred in our towns. Traditionally, the siting and construction of towns was determined in relation to the four elements. Settlers would rely on the position of the stars, or on the convergence points of the winds, or on telluric lines. Nomads would gather around a special tree, a totem or an altar. Villages were created on the site of a rock, at the foot of a hill or a magic mountain. And when there were no such points of reference, a tumulus, pyramid or cathedral would be built. It was always a question of establishing a link between a plot of land and the vastness of the Cosmos. Whatever the circumstances, the place chosen was never inert and of no consequence but would be the crossing point of magnetic forces, a kind of magical knot. Each inhabitant could feel they were at the centre of the world. The town would be endowed with a maternal and protective symbolism, a womb-like enclosure in which man was always in contact with the earth's energies and could peacefully grow towards heaven.

Today, we are very far indeed from this ancient wisdom. The old towns which have kept intact their meaningful spatial organization are very rare. During the Middle Ages, the cathedrals clearly conveyed a living message: now they seem out of place and voiceless. This absence of an identifiable reference point is at the root of our feelings of insecurity. Modern towns increase this negativity with their arbitrary perspectives, their huge parking lots, their unending underground corridors, their soulless shopping centres . . .

The intention of the builders of these modern towns has been to compartmentalize, to make a profit by dividing space into 'zones' and, by doing this excessively, they have ended up sterilizing and destroying all the subtle qualities which were once native to that space. Devoid of any symbolic reference, the geometric plans exert a negative influence on our behaviour. The only telluric lines which we still take into consideration are the channels for the circulation of merchandise, so that, overworked and confused, we have finally completely given up on any attempt at intelligent planning . . . A good example of this arbitrary planning is an American metropolis, planned without a real centre; another is the sprawling urban growth which is typical of developing countries. The result is always the same – urban violence in all its variations, a modern Babylon, the antithesis of the heavenly Jerusalem . . .

What should we do? You may say that the responsibility lies with urban planners and architects. True, but in the meantime, while waiting for them to change their world vision, we should try to reinvent our own orientation rites. In our daily movements, we should visualize a central point and then the boundaries of a city. When you walk down the street, when you go for a stroll, whether in the town or the country, you must mentally do the same thing. Make a note of features and natural boundaries, give a meaning to your path, and be sensitive to the telluric forces which are active around you. The suburban gangs understand this, as they desperately try to revitalize their depressed neighbourhoods by marking out their territory with graffiti. We should do the same symbolically with our territory, not to forbid access to it, but to inhabit it in a healthier, more creative way; not to make it sterile, but to give it all the potential of the alchemist's crucible.

The rites of orientation bring out all that is sacred in Nature: all telluric currents radiate out from a natural centre. By working with these revitalizing powers, man automatically endows his gestures with meaning and draws unseen allies to himself!

For the earth is inhabited! And not only by humans . . . Each of the elements is served by elemental spirits, who are the hidden soul of everything which exists, multi-faceted magical beings, which can behave like mischievious elves or throw titanic rages. They are the *djinns* of Muslim folklore, the *nethers* of the Egyptians, who served the Goddess Isis, and the Scandinavian elves, as well as the numerous spirits honoured by the Celts, the spirits of Gaia.

By this point, you are probably thinking that I am one of those 'enlightened' beings, who confuses various levels of reality. Cynics might ask how one can reconcile the idea of one Creator of the Whole with the ancient Celtic fairy tales. And I would reply, 'how can we know exactly what God has created?' Until just recently, we had not yet discovered the immensity of the Cosmos. Why should there not be living entities in the air, under the earth, in the waves and in fire itself? How is it that humankind, in its romantic imaginings, consistently intuited living forces in both the earth and the heavens throughout time? Only the details of these tales differ. Does this not suggest that these beings do animate the elements? Why should we feel such intense emotion before the marvels of nature, if in reality they are nothing more than a mountain, a lake, a waterfall or a volcano? You know very well that these have their own language, that they 'speak' to some other dimension in us: they communicate with a part of us which is beyond our under-standing, but which we can tune into if our rational side is quietened. To refer to these legends does not necessarily imply giving credit to old wives' tales. Sometimes, perhaps, but not always. It is no longer acceptable to think that progress means rejecting ancient knowledge; it has become just an affectation to impress others. Scientists have become much humbler and more open to other possibilities. One can see that they will have their part to play in the true progress which will take place during the Age of Aquarius. Galileo was condemned, the first healers were burnt – they were, in fact, the first doctors – and condemned as witches; the first inventors were tortured before being honoured. Today, both telepathy and other powers of perceiving 'things behind things' are the subject of scientific research. There is a growing interest in studying the type of medicine which deals with the 'energetic' body, although people still often see these techniques as slightly fanciful. But they will eventually prevail and win their place, as did the ancient art of acupuncture.

Of course, this growing acceptance of mysterious phenomena brings with it a convoy of charlatans, giving the sceptics something to be cynical about. But, for heaven's sake, let's not reject every paranormal revelation, for these could one day turn out to be completely 'normal'.

Therefore, in all humility and without fear of derision, I believe that the earth is inhabited. The undines live in the water, the gnomes inhabit the depths of the earth, the sylphs animate the air, and the salamanders feed on fire. Our ancestors were conscious of their presence and kept a place in their homes for them or made them offerings. They are benevolent spirits, but can be mischievous. The most obvious manifestation of their mischief is that they show themselves only to those who believe in their existence, to those who have retained their ability to marvel, those who have imagination, 'that quasi-divine faculty', as Baudelaire said, 'which perceives the intimate and secret relationship between things, the correspondences and analogies.' Have you never watched in fascination those supernatural beings who shimmer in the flames of a fireplace or those marvellous clouds up in the sky? We have to learn to win over those creatures and enjoy their incessant play. We could avoid so much superfluous stress, if only we knew how to recognize, in amongst our petty everyday worries, the games of gnomes or sylphs! A bunch of keys which disappears, an electrical appliance which refuses to work and then suddenly starts functioning, a door which bangs without a draft, a sudden shower coming down from a blue sky, an invisible obstacle which trips us up – instead of losing your temper and cursing these objects which plot against you, take these incidents as manifestations of these creatures.

These events are not always without significance. Try to interpret these signs, for these elemental spirits, who are at the service of higher powers, often come to help us. Naturally, they don't have the same stature as our great guides, but they can send us messages or put us back on track when we have lost our way.

I have experienced examples of this almost daily. Recently, I was contacted by a woman journalist who immediately declared that she was 'very taken with esotericism'. This kind of statement usually puts me on my guard: nothing annoys me more than spirituality 'worn on the sleeve'. It so happens that this journalist asked me to lend her a book by Jacob Boehme[12], the famous German 'mystical shoemender', who lived in the seventeenth century, an important figure in my spiritual evolution. In my book *Journey*, I related how, after a startling mystical experience, I saw a man dressed in black, who appeared out of nowhere and before vanishing again, put this book in my hand . . .

I could not possibly refuse to lend this book to someone who had expressed a desire to read it. Therefore, I looked out the book and put it on the corner of my desk. The journalist arrived, we talked for a while, then came the moment when I went to hand her the book. It had vanished into thin air. I looked everywhere but it was nowhere to be found. I apologized, but there was no way I could find it at that moment. When the journalist finished her interview, I showed her out. When I returned to my desk, I was amazed to find that the book by Boehme was back, exactly where I had put it! Had the gnomes hidden it to show me that this woman was not yet ready to receive the message the book contained?

Have fun observing the signs which the elemental spirits show you and they will, little by little, become your playmates and your accomplices, and they will constantly remind you that matter is not necessarily satanic. Nature and the objects which surround us, although apparently inanimate, have a life of their own; they all vibrate like us, and they have an aura which allows them to inter-act with us and transform raw matter. Like the poet or the alchemist, you should learn to transform mud into gold . . .

We have discussed how the gnomes, the undines, the sylphs and the salamanders are not hostile to us. Nevertheless, they have not sworn allegiance to man, but to the earth. Their mission is not so much to protect us, but to safeguard the planet. If man continues to contribute to the destruction of Gaia, as he is doing at present, these cheerful tricksters could become merciless monsters. By our destructive and polluting behaviour, we are going to force them to take severe measures. Already, there are many warning signs; the gnomes provoke ever more frequent earthquakes, the undines multiply the floods as well as the droughts, the salamanders wake the volcanoes and light gigantic forest fires, and the sylphs make the hurricanes blow and cause aeroplanes to crash . . . We are caught in a spiral of destruction: we pillage Gaia and the elemental spirits take their revenge, but they also build up a negative karma which collectively we will have to pay off in addition to our individual karmic debts.

The blue planet is now disfigured, unrecognizable. It has become the *Hyle*[13] of the Gnostics, that degraded land which is like an anti-Eden. By wanting to play at being sorcerer's apprentices, man has put the earth's natural equilibrium in peril. Logically, if he does not mend his ways, he will suffer the consequences of his acts. 'By cutting wood in lieu of the Great Carpenter, clever is the one who does not hurt himself,' said Lao Tsu. Why do we not listen to the great Chinese sage?

> Whoever wants to take hold of the world and use it
> Is bound to fail.
> The world is a sacred vase
> Which does not tolerate being possessed or used.
> Whoever uses it, destroys it,
> Whoever holds it, loses it.
>
> *Tao Te Ching* (Ch 29)

These verses echo the biblical words which I quoted in my book *The End of Time*. 'The time has come to judge the dead and to destroy those who destroy the earth,' it says in the Revelation of St John. And in Isaiah 33: 1: 'Woe to you, destroyer, who yourself have not been destroyed; you treacherous one, with whom none has dealt treacherously! When you have ceased to destroy, you will be destroyed.'

It is futile to recite again the long list of degradations to which our modern folly has submitted Gaia. We know only too well the terrible litany of disasters: devastated forests, dying rivers, seas which have become dumping sites for waste, the chemical contamination of soils, natural resources stretched to the limit, the nuclear menace, the polluted atmosphere . . . For more details, I would refer the reader to my two previous books or to the newspapers which report daily on this agony, unimaginable only a century ago, for those who had not read the ancient prophecies contained in the Bible and other sacred books . . .

I would, therefore, like to go back to a subject which has tended to become taboo, perhaps because it is, in my view, the root of all these evils: a galloping population explosion. It was not until the middle of the nineteenth century that the earth's population reached a billion individuals. At present, that same number of people is born in just one decade! We number six billion and in another generation or two, there will be a further four billion on this planet. The scientists all agree that beyond that point, the planet is no longer viable. It has already been said, in the *Mahabarata*, the Sanskrit epic which was written several centuries before Jesus Christ (12th Song, 248: 13–17): 'The annihilation of the human race will take place when the Creator finds no other solution but the total destruction of the world to put an end to the disastrous and unplanned multiplication of human beings.'

We need look no further than the colossal increase in the world's population to find the cause of all destruction, because it has become necessary to build more, to clear land, to consume more, to fight over plots of earth . . . Since the end of the Second World War, we have built seas of concrete buildings, and monstrous towers have sprung up like mushrooms. I say monstrous because while vertical architecture is ideal for offices, it is a disaster as far as quality of life is concerned. Unfortunately, the other current solution is not really an improvement in the long term. It consists of building housing estates that spread their tentacles out into the countryside. It is a more humanized option, but horizontal urbanization means encroaching on agricultural land which then becomes scarce. The planet covered by individual homes, the age of the housing estate! And this evil will become complete when there are no longer any wild animals, forests, or agriculture . . .

How can we ignore the fact that the only way of solving the problem for the future lies in stemming this suicidal global increase in births? I know that it is a difficult subject – taboo, in fact.

Because some people see birth control as an attack on their individual freedom and others see it as going against the command to 'go forth and multiply'. People are horrified when they learn that the Chinese government takes draconian measures to limit the number of children that each family is allowed, overlooking the fact that for China it is a question of avoiding widespread famine. Not so very long ago French politicians urged people to 'have children, have children, otherwise who will pay for your retirement pensions?', but we are beginning to realize, in the global village era, that we should not heed that advice, especially since soon there won't be any more pensions . . .

The danger of worldwide overpopulation has begun to dawn on aware people. But many remain oblivious to it, for this information has not reached certain civilizations and cultures, where sectarian religions remain inflexible. And I don't just mean Muslim countries or those of the Third World! We have in Rome a Pope who stubbornly refuses to accept any form of contraception and for whom this creed of 'proliferation' remains a must. But we always pay for our mistakes in the end: 'The fools and the mad behave like enemies towards themselves, performing evil deeds whose fruit is bitter,' says the *Dhammapada*, one of the major Buddhist texts.

In spite of our blinkered attitude, we know that we cannot go on at the present rate. Gaia is a living organism who will react in order to ensure her survival. She possesses a great number of weapons with which to attack man if attitudes do not change. To defend herself, she can concoct terrible new illnesses, linked to sex and reproduction. It is quite justifiable for the planet to limit the growth of a destructive humanity, using even the most devastating measures, like a third world war or a collision with a comet . . .

Must we therefore resign ourselves to the inevitability of the coming disasters? Should we wait to be decimated to be reborn? Or should we admit, with regards to overpopulation particularly, that although a voluntary reduction of births would perhaps represent a restraint of individual liberty, it would be for the good of all.

Sooner or later, we will have to differentiate between the individual and the human being. The individual is only a small conditioned entity, who revolves around an egotistical self, protected by little gods and petty traditions. On the other hand, the human being, as a divine creature, feels responsible for the whole world, for its well-being and for its confusion. 'Every man should say: it is for me that the world has been created and I take responsibility for it,' says a Jewish proverb (Sanhedrin 37b).

We won't be able to escape: this realization is the *sine qua non* condition for the emergence of a new era, which will only happen if, according to the Indian sage Krishnamurti, 'each of us recognizes the central fact that we individuals, as human beings, wherever we are and to whatever culture we belong, are totally responsible for the general state of the world'. That means that each of us, because of our prejudices and self-centred aggression, is responsible for every conflict. People are becoming increasingly conscious of this fact intellectually, but for a real change to take place, they have to feel and experience it in their hearts.

To accept that responsibility does not mean to take on a heavy burden of guilt. On the contrary, it is an entirely positive stand: to take responsibility is also to give oneself the power to act. I am not so big-headed as to think that I could find a cure for all the ills of the planet, but I do insist on the fact that each of us, in his or her individual behaviour, can and should contribute to the necessary reconciliation between man and Gaia. When they are not incompetent, our politicians and world-leaders are overwhelmed with work: we cannot wait for them to decide for us and solve our problems. Our behaviour should justify our right to vote and is our means of deliverance.

The first thing to do is to put a stop to our greed. People in rich countries should not listen to the constant encouragements to consume more. Far from being a panacea, development at any price only speeds our headlong fall into the void. We have to modify our habits so as to reduce waste and squandering, curtail our excessive production, and learn frugality. It is not a question of 'tightening our belts', but of realizing that we are living under a regime which encourages excess. It is estimated that today, one fifth of humanity disposes of four fifths of the earth's riches. In terms of commercial energy consumption, one North American consumes as much as 140 Bangladeshis, or 280 inhabitants of Chad or Haiti . . . Their needs are not the same, we might say, but does that give rich countries the right to dissipate our global inheritance? A native of Haiti or Chad is 'worth' exactly the same as a European, no more no less. And if we really want to avoid disaster, we will have to work hard at solidarity and sharing. Running water has become something that many take for granted; we use it and abuse it, whereas one person in three in the world suffers from appalling droughts. The same goes for our food and energy resources. Sooner or later, governments will have to increase taxes on water dramatically, as well as on other natural resources, which are becoming scarce. Why not preempt and prevent that move, both at home and at work, by controlling our tendency to waste these resources? Do you know that the meat-producing countries use more cereals to feed their animals than the whole of the Third World consumes? When we understand how harmful meat is for spiritual equilibrium, we begin to wonder if a change of diet would not do us a world of good . . .

It is by changing individual behaviour that we will reduce the three major imbalances which undermine the planet: between North and South, between rich and poor, and between man and Nature.

To preserve the earth as well as to purify our inner selves, we once again need to find the appropriate behaviour, that which corresponds to our real necessities and does not interfere with divine order. 'May the sage live in his village like the bee collects its nectar, without spoiling the flower in its colour or perfume,' says the Dhammapada.

Thinking that all this is useless and could not possibly influence the future of the world is unjustifiable. Great revolutions have always started off with personal initiatives. In the same way, I am perhaps only a drop of water in the ocean, but if that drop is pure, it can purify what is around it. A spiritual quest is not egotistical; it implies not only saving oneself, but also uplifting others. The challenge of the third millennium is enormous; it is about attempting universal reintegration with the laws of the Cosmos.

Today, the intensification of vibrations and the flux of invisible energies invite us to bring about this change of attitude. We are becoming increasingly aware that, in spite of man's crimes, the earth is trying to ascend to a higher and purer level of consciousness, and that we will have to follow that movement. That vibrational change is visible in the animal, vegetable and mineral realms. I see it every single day: the animals are joyful, the birds sing like never before. The dolphins and the whales are coming closer to humans . . . who find nothing better to do than to massacre them. In the forests, where I often stroll, I am enchanted to find that the deer also come close . . . so long as one is not surrounded by negative vibrations. If you smoke or drink excessively – which means that you are still the prisoner of a self-destructive rationale – they will avoid you. But animals are now experiencing the colossal joy of knowing that a new stage of consciousness is in the making, a new harmonious order is approaching. To participate in this, man has to be reconciled with Nature. He would be doing no more than following the general movement described in the Song of Songs: first the bewilderment, then the crisis and finally, we hope, the reunion. We should remember that the earth does not belong to man, but man to the earth. And if we insist on this power struggle, we must know that we don't stand a chance of winning . . .

You will, no doubt, tell me that collective responsibility concerning the earth and feeling part of the Cosmos are hard to comprehend when daily we have to deal with the restrictions of the everyday routine of 'travel–work–sleep'. Nevertheless, Lao Tsu is right when he recommends: 'Don't consider your native abode too narrow, don't abhore the condition into which you were born. One does not feel disgust, unless one allows oneself to' (*Tao Te*

Ching, Ch 72). Running away won't reawaken our sense of wonder and help us find our place in the Cosmos. Let's content ourselves, as Plotinus says, to flee towards 'our dear homeland': 'Our homeland is the place we come from and our Father is there. For that voyage, we need not prepare a carriage, nor any ship, but we must stop looking and, closing our eyes, exchange that way of seeing for another, and awaken that faculty which everyone possesses, but few make use of.'

That faculty is, once again, meditation. 'Without going out of the door, we can know the whole world; without looking out of the window, we can understand the ways of heaven,' confirms the *Tao Te Ching*. Therefore we should take up meditation to calm the mind that constantly fragments our perceptions, masking the unity of the Universe. Adopt a meditation position, and go within yourself to explore the limits of your body with your mind. Do the rounds of your physical reality. Then visualize your body, and see yourself becoming smaller and smaller, going deeper within yourself. Your chest can then become an immense vault into which the energies descend. You open up and expand to encompass the whole Cosmos. Now that you know the practice, it can be more than just a mental picture, as it was when you only wanted to calm your spirit; it's a real experience. You are in a state of osmosis with the whole, the oneness of creation – not yet with God Himself, who is much more difficult to reach, but you're on the way!

To help you attain that stage, you can resort to the technique of prayer while breathing in: recite the prayer mentally when inhaling and totally let yourself go when exhaling. By doing so, you are imitating the fundamental law of the Cosmos, which is the alternating rhythm between contraction and expansion.

When you have mastered this exercise, you will be approaching a feeling of wonder – not yet the ecstasy which divine illumination induces, but a childlike sense of wonder which reveals the deeper meaning of things, opening up a magical dimension, the miraculous side of the world. You will discover, or rediscover, the unity of Nature, known to the hermeticists and alchemists, and today largely confirmed by science – that the one is contained in the whole and the whole is the one. Basil Valentine, a major alchemist of the fifteenth century wrote: 'All things come from the same seed, they were all originally born by the same Mother.'

The Western way of thinking has made us lose sight of the notion that the world is one. And if we have been able to destroy our environment in such an unconscious manner, it is primarily because we have forgotten – or pretended to forget – that we are an intrinsic part of it. A Sufi sage, when trying to explain what his religion consisted of, said: 'The Sufi does not consider his own exterior and interior, but looks at everything as pertaining to God.' If we perceive the world in its unity, we will be filled with wonder and we will then be able to intuit what could be called the law of causality, or the great architect of the Universe, the Divine, God . . .

When internally you have experienced the idea of belonging to the whole of creation, you will no longer look at Nature in the same way. You will no longer see the landscape with the eyes of a tourist. You will give things their true 'name'. In Genesis, God allowed man to name things. What does that mean? It means knowing them, approaching their secret nature, becoming conscious that all things created are a gift of God, a work of mercy. Divinity is present all around us and thus the world is a source of joy. As the great Persian poet Rumi wrote:

> All the atoms which people the air and the desert
> Know that they are enamoured like us
> And that each atom, happy or unhappy,
> Is dazzled by the sun of the universal soul.

I was lucky to have a grandmother who taught me that sense of 'voyeurism'. Passionate about magic, she repeated incessantly: 'Look, observe . . . The spirit of God is behind each object. Each thing has a reason for existing, a meaning; each object is a symbol and reflects the Universe . . . Everything is connected,' she used to tell me. That kind of attentive contemplation makes one conscious

that the material world, with its changeable façade, simultaneously hides and reveals another reality. Like Gérard de
Nerval[14], we should make the effort to pass 'trembling, through the
doors made of ivory or horn which separate us from the invisible'.

We belong to a culture which attaches enormous importance to
the visual appearance of things. But it is a media-based kind of
vision which mostly flatters our basic instincts with sensational
images. Whereas the wonder to which I am referring is the very
opposite of this, encompassing the extraordinary and the most
ordinary. The capacity to marvel becomes a daily event, lived
constantly, without ceremony or ritual. It is what Zen Buddhism
expresses in the following formula: 'At first mountains are
mountains and rivers are rivers. Then mountains are no longer
mountains and rivers are no longer rivers', which translated means
that we intellectualize and romanticize them 'but finally, the
mountains are once again mountains and rivers are once more
rivers'. In other words, and perhaps for us more clearly expressed,
it is as a Christian monk says, for whom 'the contemplative person
is not the one who discovers secrets which are unknown to others,
but the one who becomes ecstatic about what everyone knows.'

In short, the initiate can content himself with what the Universe
offers, which is to say that he will find fulfilment in what Nature
generously offers. To live in harmony with the Cosmos, with the
whole of creation, is also a way of living happily. On condition, of
course, that we know how to contemplate, to take advantage
of what is offered and to leave, as often as possible, the frantic hell
of our short-term ambitions behind.

To be in harmony with the Cosmos means, in effect, to respect the
cycles which govern and animate it. The first of these cycles is
the one which governed the creation of the world – activity and
then rest. Breathing in and out, the ebb and flow . . .

Therefore, Genesis encourages us to sanctify the seventh day of
the week in honour of our Lord, 'for he rested after his work
of creation'. A sign of the link between God and man, on the 'day

of the Lord', or the Sabbath for the Jews, we stop to catch our breath, to find the 'breath of life' once again. It is a time for us to renew our tired nerves, purify our body and find ourselves again. Weekends dedicated to catching up on paperwork, to over-eating, to motorway madness (or alternatively stuck in traffic jams), is not the most fruitful way of renewing our energies. One of the first precepts established in Exodus for the day of the Lord was that: 'Each person should stay where they are, nobody should leave their home on the seventh day.' This does not mean in the literal sense of barricading yourself in your house, but rather to give some time to your inner space and to re-orienting yourself in the world.

To live in harmony with the rhythm of the Cosmos should also mean following the cycle of the seasons. Sadly this has become increasingly difficult. Electricity has delivered us from the constraints of daylight and darkness and the passage from a rural to an urban civilization has considerably lessened our respect for the changes in the seasons, a notion which was crucial to our ancestors' lives. I know that one cannot force modern men and women to go to bed with the chickens. Try, nevertheless, to go to bed earlier in winter, and you'll see that you will reap immense benefits from following nature's rhythm, during the long nights of the cold season. During the summer, get up with the sun and meditate at dawn; your energy will multiply tenfold.

And if you find yourself regaining a taste for seasonal festivals, why not celebrate the old customs that were used to mark the changing seasons? The Jewish people celebrate Pesach, the festival of unleavened bread in the spring, Shavuot which commemorates the first wheat harvest in the summer, and the harvest festival or Sukkot, the Feast of the Tabernacles, in the autumn. All of these symbolize a joining of cosmic, earthly and human rhythms . . .

All these festivals are a way of participating in this harmonization with the Cosmos! Apart from rural customs, all religions have their feasts, usually linked to events from their sacred history. The word festival comes from the Latin *festum* which implies solemnity.

It means a day or a period consecrated to God. The calendar thus is parallel with breathing – people eaten up by anguish or by overwork are given the opportunity to regenerate themselves.

Unfortunately, many of these religious festivals have become simple celebrations, whereas they should be opportunities to recreate the original energies. To take part in a traditional festival is to enter a vast cosmic dance, to get away from meaningless routine and to recontact our desire for spiritual elevation.

A festival is symbolic of rebirth, reflected generally by the custom of wearing new clothes or by the inversion of the roles we play in daily life: the fool becomes wise, the rich become poor and vice versa. We throw away old habits, we try to look at the world with new eyes, to try to find a different way of life.

So don't despise your pleasure. Take advantage of these festivities to chase away the old you. Put down your luggage, throw away your rubbish, jump into that fountain of youth which will allow you to face tomorrow with renewed energy.

Both spiritually and psychologically, the festival is an occasion for renewal. Its playful aspect allows us to exorcise our inner demons. Its exuberance is a kind of catharsis, thanks to which we can avoid – paradoxically – floundering into excess in our daily life, for it harmonizes us with cosmic energy. Revelry is not necessarily synonymous with barbaric paganism or with drunken football hooliganism. It is about participating in the joy and wonder of creation.

A spiritual quest does not imply a serious or overheavy attitude. On the contrary, it should gradually bring us joy and liveliness. People around us will be the first to benefit – and heaven knows they need it! And this in turn will benefit us. We seem to have forgotten that we have been created, as has the Cosmos, by a loving will. And if we manage to retrieve our sense of wonder before the marvel of creation, this can help us live and survive on our planet; and then we will be rewarded, for we will have learned how to make use of love.

6

Making Use of Love

❧

It is love I want, not sacrifice.
JESUS CHRIST

Making use of love? The expression will shock a good many people, I suppose. How come? For many people this emotion means attachment, dependence, even sacrifice ('I have sacrificed myself for him, her, my children, my family, my friends), so how can we make use of it? Real Love is a powerful weapon in our struggle for balance, strength, success and happiness here on earth. But, you will notice I said 'real' Love, with a capital 'L'. Sensitive souls beware – this kind of Love will in no way fit in with cosy sentiment! However, it will fulfil us completely, in every possible way.

It is commonly said that love is beyond words. We haphazardly love our mother, our husband, our friends, the sea, carrots . . . And when we want to talk about love, human love, 'true' love, we become lost in a maze of confused, difficult feelings. Physical attraction, sexual passion, married love, filial affection, parental love, brotherly love, friendship, charity – all these are connected with love. But do we know how to love, and do we know how to find fulfilment in it?

Don't expect me to say that sexual desire is wrong. It is a divine gift, as are all the pleasures of the senses which Nature offers.

When we fall in love, we are filled with wild enthusiasm, a burst of energy lifts our spirits. These feelings are more than just the pulsation of life: the attraction between two people allows for intense moments of joy and physical communion, and furthermore it touches on a primordial memory of a time when we were androgynous beings.

Unfortunately, desire often proves ephemeral and purely sensual love leaves us with a feeling of insufficiency and incompleteness. Naturally, it is a side of our nature that we should explore, even if there is the risk of slipping into debauchery . . . We know that many saints have trodden that path, until the day they realized that these excesses left a bitter taste in the mouth and that perhaps carnal desire had another purpose, reminding us of a higher, suprahuman need.

We are not there yet: once again, we are not saints. But we have all learned to differentiate between being 'in love' and the love we have for those who are particularly dear to us. No doubt, to feel true love for a man or a woman means to be 'in love' with them but more so. And in the other forms of love where sex is not involved, we have a tendency to believe that our love is 'pure' and, above all, disinterested.

Desire wants to possess, love gives: at least, that is what we claim. But we know very well that in practice that is not always the way it works. Unconsciously, instinctively, we want our dear ones to be what we expect them to be. We criticize our parents, because their behaviour is not in accordance with our wishes. We expect our spouse to be a faithful companion, matching our ideal, refusing them the right to be their own person or treating them like slaves, making them indispensable to us, which comes to much the same thing. Many mothers and fathers see their children as an extension of their own selves, forgetting that, if we believe in reincarnation, tomorrow we will have another life, another family, other descendants. Many parents feel hurt when their children do not want to follow them into business or when they don't want to practise the profession chosen for them. Parents often put their children to shame if they don't live up to their expectations. We sometimes close the door of friendship saying, 'he's neglected me, I can't accept his attitude, he didn't help me when I needed it'. Sometimes, when we speak of colleagues, friends or bosses with whom we have to share a great part of our time, sometimes even being passionately involved with them, we say, thoughtlessly, 'After all I did for them!' . . . before sulking in a corner, feeling sorry for ourselves, wounded by so much ingratitude.

In short, if we manage to relate – albeit only on a temporary basis – to pagan Eros, who presides not just over sensuality, but also over our drive to excel, we don't seem to have any talent for Agape, brotherly love, loving the other without expecting anything in return. That's human, you may say; we are neither perfect, nor that generous. The trouble is, when we are the loved one, we dearly hope to be cherished in that way: with respect for our freedom, with indulgence, kindness and fidelity, expecting nothing in return!

No wonder, among such a mass of contradictions, the poet should exclaim: 'There is no such thing as happy love'.

But if there is no such thing as a happy love, it's our fault! We expect from love a perfection that only God can give. That's our great mistake! But don't misunderstand me – I'm not suggesting that we become absorbed in worship to compensate us for our human failings, but simply that we avail ourselves of Divine Love to make up for our lack, so that we can love and be loved better here on earth, without having to go through pointless suffering or making others suffer.

This is the first step, for we will see how 'making use of love' has many other advantages, on our travels here on earth and on our journey towards heaven.

What do we expect from earthly love, fools that we are? Total understanding and sharing. That is to say the impossible. Other people just don't understand – our efforts to please them, the wounds they inflict on us, sometimes unknowingly, our secret wishes which we feel they should be able to guess, our personal anguishes (as if they did not have theirs), our hopes, our despair. What about sharing? They are completely selfish (and we are not!), thinking about their own worries, as we ponder over ours, never having time for us and, above all, revealing themselves incapable of making decisions. Complaints about this sort of love have been sung, written and cried about throughout history.

And yet, in our loneliness, a divine presence, with all the love in the world, remains at our disposal. A unique love, and even in our extreme jealousy we can accept sharing it with others, because we know that it is available for each and everyone of us. Of course, I am speaking of God's love.

So, while waiting for this Divine Love to teach us how to use our feelings here on earth, we can take refuge in Him, and find there an indescribable source of comfort.

Needless to say, it is not a question of cutting oneself off from the world, as certain misanthropists do in the hope of setting themselves apart from the 'masses' and becoming part of the elect. It is enough to search, not for beatitude, but for this supra-terrestrial happiness which will quench our thirst for the absolute.

You will find that happiness by practising meditation, the prayer from the heart, the most gratifying prayer of all.

Meditation of the heart begins with waiting. One puts oneself into a state of expectant adoration, during which anything can happen. The mind is calm, and the inner turmoil is swept away; we don't ask for anything, there is just pure prayer, a receptive vibration which has the powerful imprint of our needs and our weaknesses, of that tremendous void created by our need for love. An inescapable natural law ordains that every vibration attracts a response of a similar intensity. If we really remain intensely expectant, in all humility, the radiation of Divine Love will descend towards us. Communication is then established: the fourth chakra (the heart chakra) is activated. A sensation of heat will be felt in the heart region. Not like a burn, which would consume us, but a soft warmth: we literally 'warm our hearts'.

An immense joy can then be felt, a joy which makes us suddenly realize that, wherever we may be, prey to misfortune or in the middle of the most terrifying desert, we are never alone. The higher powers answer us and we are overwhelmed. For it is that unexpected vibration which, if sustained, carries us to a state of rapture. Meditation of the heart transforms us into 'anointed' beings. We are overcome by a huge wave of tenderness, we welcome it into the innermost recesses of our soul and we feel gratified.

That vibration is feminine; it is the vibration of the original Holy Trinity from which the Virgin was not excluded. It is ineffably sweet and it plunges us into a state of delicious abandon, that abandon which we rarely dare indulge in among humans, even, and above all, in close relationships, where the games of competition, the need to be found attractive, and possessiveness all come into play. That Love sweeps away forever our fear of not being loved. How reassuring! We know at last that we are accepted as we are. God does not love us because we more or less deserve it. He loves us completely and without reservation.

Let us not forget to be grateful to Him for that! For at last, we who begged, implored and obtained considerable benefits from His help, have also known joy through Him. That deserves appreciation and thankfulness!

This experience might allow us to love others, without asking for anything in return – at least not in the name of love. Having experienced Divine Love, we become overwhelmed with compassion for humanity. Are other people not just like us – solitary, vulnerable, begging for healing tenderness? We feel the need to share that joy with which we are suddenly brimming over. It is up to us not to reject that feeling when we begin to fear that showing such generosity might make us lose out in the jungle of our petty professional or family quarrels.

We live in a hard, merciless universe. I'm sure we all agree on that. In our working life, in our relationships, whether parental, marital or filial, we sometimes have to dominate, impose our views, expose cheating, reveal traps, win. And many among you will no doubt think that in such circumstances, even if the meditation-rapture has made you conscious of the humbling similarity between all human beings, it is not appropriate to be seen to be sentimental.

But, who is talking of sentimentality here? Is God sentimental? No, He is benevolent, which means that He looks on us with love and that He does not wish us any harm. If we follow His example, we will find great reserves of strength – in our work, among our family, in our friendships, in our relationships with others. Look at the enormous waste of energy caused by your negative attitudes towards rivals, enemies and any other kind of opponents. Think about the irritation you feel when others don't agree with you or if they challenge your judgment. If you see them as God's creatures, just like yourself, endowed with the same freedom that God has given you, including that of not giving in to all your desires, you will save a precious amount of time – the time spent in self-centred rebellion, whims and childish tantrums. Time wasted being morally indignant without having valid reasons for doing so, sharpening your weapons, in case of a fight. Furthermore, if you can see those you talk with as being much the same as yourself, you are more likely to be able to see their true motivations and avoid being manipulated by them. To follow the example of that love with God shows us is to erase all the prejudices which prevent us from seeing clearly. This does not mean becoming a docile victim, but rather coping better with conflict and being able to defend oneself, as in a sports competition – in honest combat, where one knows the adversary but feels no hatred for him, and does not judge him.

The holy scriptures say, 'Thou shalt not judge' and that we should leave that difficult task to God. Someone whom we may find hateful is at most someone who is mistaken. Ask God to put him or her back on the right path. Does that person wish to harm us? We should not waste our energy cursing their bad intentions. We can prepare for confrontation by taking advantage of the law of non-resistance which is recommended by the sacred texts. There again, these are often misunderstood. Christ's terrible demand in

Matthew 5: 38–39, has always been considered controversial: 'You have heard that it was said, "An eye for an eye and a tooth for a tooth." But I say to you, Do not resist one who is evil. But if anyone strikes you on the right cheek, turn to him the other also.' The Gospel tries, in this case, to make us understand that if we don't react to aggression with aggression, our adversary will be put off balance, for that is not what he is expecting. Biblical tradition speaks of the same principle, and when it says 'Bless your enemy and you deprive him of his arrows', it is not inciting vengeful hypocrisy. It simply means that if we don't confront irrational violence with open animosity, our opponent loses balance. This in no way means that we should not stand up for our rights. In fact, it is the equivalent of putting into practice top quality mental judo.

If a friend storms into my home, looking for a quarrel because of some rumour he has heard, I refuse to enter the discussion and thereby prevent the dispute from escalating. Is he angry? I listen attentively to his complaints. If necessary, I recognize my faults. 'If you're saying that I acted like that, it is no doubt true. I was unaware that my behaviour was so bad. I beg your pardon. If it made you feel that way, you must be right.' Miraculously, his rage dissolves – even though he had come to declare war. We then talk calmly and achieve reconciliation. So many times I have disarmed people's aggression by refusing to allow my ego to take control. There is a basic natural law that when a strong wave comes to the shore, it will explode violently if it hits a rock, but will die calmly on a beach . . .

I remember my mother often repeated this Spanish proverb: 'Two people cannot quarrel when one of them does not want to . . .' A proverb echoed by this Zen saying: 'What noise can one hand make?' Every time we are confronted by conflict, whether at home or at work, before getting on our high horse, we should try to admit that we may well have played a role, even if indirectly, in creating that situation.

The Buddha insists that we should 'Vanquish rage with love, evil with good. Conquer the miser with generosity, the liar with truth.'

We have a lot to gain by practising benevolent neutrality. Meditation, in all its forms, will help us achieve that. Thanks to our inner purification and to the love which the higher powers bestow on us when we pray from the heart, we will learn to love ourselves. And if we love ourselves, we will be much less susceptible to outer enmities. Christ said 'Love your neighbour as you love yourself.' Therefore, if you learn to love yourself, you will also love those around you.

In the Lord's Prayer we ask God: 'Forgive us our trespasses, as we forgive those who trespass against us.' And that, I would agree with you, is even more difficult. When we have been really hurt, we feel like taking revenge. But what a worry, what a waste of time! Have we ourselves never made anyone suffer by our own obstinacy? Then, let us forgive! Even if we feel forced and constrained to do so by the sacred texts, we should still forgive! Think of the inner freedom you will discover, which you can then apply to other tasks. To plot revenge takes days, months, years . . . Imagine how light you will feel and how much stronger, if you give up wasting your vital energy on rancour. You don't have to see your enemies again; in fact, it would be in your interest not to have anything to do with them, so forget them!

Furthermore, we must realize that the sacred texts are not just manuals for family or work management. Not harming others, even if we hold a grudge against them, but, above all, forgiving them is a way to lighten our karma, or at the least not make it any heavier.

The prayer of love which so overwhelmed us – does it not suggest that other people need kindness rather than aggression, just as we do? Should we wait until they are all loveable, attractive and perfect before we start loving them? The task of the initiate is to guide the ignorant towards brotherhood.

The end of the Piscean Age is marked by an insatiable need for love, amidst the generalized contempt with which the individual is treated. Traumatized by our anonymity among the crowd, lost in an ant-like civilization, we increasingly suffer from a feeling of non-existence. Many young people try to compensate for this by going around in gangs, or by attending rock concerts or sports events with almost religious fervour. But for some, their suffering is so great that they are ready to do anything to draw attention to themselves, including acts of violence.

Those people, often themselves victims of neglect, who take up fanatical totalitarian activities, are also a good example of this thirst for recognition. They find in those movements a means of identifying with something, a refuge from a world where the general 'non-sense' makes them feel lost. These movements provide an opportunity for them to do something and escape the disdain of society.

To banish contempt for others should be one of the first tasks of the initiate. The theory of reincarnation can help in this. It puts forward in no uncertain terms the fact that our sex, our colour and our social status have nothing whatsoever to do with the state of our soul. I said as much in the introduction to this book. One can hold an important position and carry the most terrible karma, while a beggar can be further evolved than the person who gives him alms. Even intelligence is not an indication of nobility where the evolution of the soul is concerned. It is a fine attribute to have of course, but intelligence is often at the mercy of rationality and, therefore, can be the ideal home for satanic powers. If we think about it, intelligence is only a faculty which allows us to adapt, an aid to double-dealing. The true key for spiritual growth is not the capacity to play mind games, but simplicity. We should choose Sufism, rather than sophism.

In any case, once we understand the law which governs the trans-migration of souls, we will never again look down condescendingly on those who seem to be in an inferior position socially.

By doing so, we take the sting out of countless power struggles. If we can really look at our fellow men – even those who are strangers to our environment – from that perspective, our attitude will change. Instead of turning away from those we consider to be different from ourselves, why not pay more attention to them and be more open to them? One of the surest ways of developing a sense of brotherhood (bearing in mind that all human beings are God's creatures) is constantly to renew our curiosity about the infinite variety of human faces. That variety is a blessing and a wonder, surprising though that may seem. Working in fashion, I believe I know how to recognize beauty, be it classical or exotic. There is the obvious beauty of the top models which we can all appreciate. But in the street, in restaurants, on public transport, we encounter that beauty which without exception is present in every face. I have been observing people for years and have come to certain conclusions, which I mention in my first book *Journey*: certain features, such as the size of the ear lobes or the placement of the pupils, provide precious information about a person's real 'age'. For there are old souls, who have already lived through many existences, and there are young souls, who are living their first incarnation. For me, they are equally important. God has offered us the natural world to contemplate, but in my view, the greatest gift He has given us is the myriad faces we can see around us, all different, all beautiful. Ugliness does not exist – or perhaps it does, but only as an aspect of beauty. If you want to become familiar with the great family of humanity, start by observing this sublime and infinite work of art. Our cities, which have become increasingly cosmopolitan, are an unending source of discovery. The face, the only part of the body which is always naked, is the first thing we notice about another person, and its vulnerability is the same as ours, inviting closeness.

For that is what brotherhood is about – closeness. The 'communion' of the early Christians, coming together as one body, symbolizes human reconciliation within the community; this is the full realization of the individual's humanity. That attitude is celebrated in the Buddhist *Suttanipata* as the best mode of existence:

> Just as a mother keeps watch and protects her only child, risking her
> life, so should we, with a boundless spirit, cherish all living things
> and love the whole world, below and above and around, without

limitation, with benevolent and infinite beauty. While upright or walking, sitting or lying down, as long as we are awake we should cultivate this thought. This is the supreme way of living.

Brotherhood means compassion, and is demanded by the Koran as well as the Judaeo-Christian and the Oriental sacred texts. It is to understand and to share in mankind's distress, at least morally. We cannot relieve all the ills of the world, but we can at least try not to close our doors but instead practise sympathy and receptiveness.

In all religions, hospitality is presented as a divine virtue. There is no doubt that we should cultivate it and revive it. Curiously, in Latin there is a phonetic link, and perhaps an etymological one as well, between *hostis* and *hospes*, enemy and host, as if to emphasize that civilization took a decisive step forward when an enemy or a stranger became a guest. In ancient times the arrival of a traveller was taken as the sign of a blessing from heaven, a good omen from the gods.

We cannot give shelter to all the poor, but we can make the effort to develop certain qualities in ourselves; we can become more receptive and available to others. Do we know how to welcome others at home or at work? 'Welcoming' does not necessarily mean offering shelter and food; it primarily means observing and, above all, listening. People today are lost in contradictions and complexity; they are looking for someone who will listen and they need to talk. The churches have failed, so there are no longer confessors. Therefore, each of us has to develop that ability to listen.

For deep down, what we pompously call 'charity' or even 'altruism', means above all to offer others our attention. We should go before them knowing that we are fellow-travellers in that fragile 'fishing boat' as Nostradamus called it. I know that our evolution and our destinies are indissolubly linked. We cannot be content to evolve 'each for himself', for apart from every man's personal karma, we have come to earth to take upon ourselves humanity's collective karma, the sum of all human actions. If I have chosen to incarnate physically into this society, at this particular historical moment, it is because the positive and negative qualities of contemporary men are also mine. I am part of this karma and, therefore, must apply my efforts to help in the evolution of my contemporaries.

We mentioned above that what makes modern man suffer most at the moment is the feeling that he does not exist in other people's eyes, and that is the cause of many a conflict. I have often had the opportunity of observing this, sitting on the terrace of a well-known Parisian café in Les Halles, a central terminus for many trains coming from the suburbs. Hundreds of people file past, of all ages, alone or in groups. They all have the same anxious look, seeking another pair of eyes, looking for a stranger who will be friendly and not see them as curiosities. One of the great crimes which modernity has committed is to have taken away or suppressed the equivalent of the Greek *agora*. This was the meeting place where people could assemble and exchange points of view. Thus, the immense solitude of the modern urban masses renders them more than ready to listen to and follow the first leader who might wish to manipulate them.

Without being patronizing, which would be against my most basic principles, I observe them with tenderness. Some smile at me, others recognize me, and some approach me and ask me for an autograph. I occasionally invite people to have a drink and I can see in their eyes how that simple invitation moves and revives them. One of my elegant clients, who does not mind travelling by metro, told me how one day she felt faint on the Underground platform, and she asked a young Indian man to help her towards the exit. 'When I took the arm he was offering me, I saw such joy in his eyes,' she told me. She's not young, so she was not trying to boast about her charms. She was just marvelling at how simple it is to offer someone a moment of joy: by treating as an equal somebody who is used to being treated as an inferior.

Compassion is one of the essential pillars of the alchemist's quest. 'If you want to realize yourself,' writes Basil Valentine in *The*

Labyrinth of the Twelve Keys, 'be without sin, persevere in Virtue. May your spirit be enlightened with the love of Light and Truth. Make the resolution, after having acquired the divine gift that you desire, to extend a hand to the poor who are bogged down in the mud, to help and lift those who are in distress.'

We have to be wary of false charity, that which we practise to assuage our guilt, or to make us feel good. You must have seen people who, when leaving a church or some other religious place, immediately readopt their aggressive attitude, pushing others out of the way, sometimes even insulting them. I know we are not supposed to leave a church in a state of perfection, but if it has that little effect on us, we would be wasting less time going to a bar!

We should not give charity of any kind just to appease fate or to satisfy our pride or to feel 'good'; nor should we do it for show, even less to lighten our karma. God is not a cash register. If we do 'good' just to earn 'indulgences' and pass to higher vibrational levels, this will not be taken into account. The reward will not be ours unless our intentions are truly generous and disinterested. Matthew 5: 3 tells us: 'But when you give alms, do not let your left hand know what your right hand is doing.'

We should not practise charity by pompously pretending to educate people whom we consider spiritually undeveloped. That is a common temptation for those who consider themselves to be well on the way to knowledge. Oriental wisdom warns us: 'He who believes he is on the path to Tao, is not on the path to Tao.' A Jewish proverb says: 'The sage is not he who pretends to know, but he who is capable of learning from any man.' Approaching others with the attitude that we are exceptional and wonderful is sure to make them want to run away.

Another mistake to avoid in our attempts to be generous, is to use this practice to exorcise fear. To try to tame urban gangs by showing a timid sympathy for them in order to avoid being attacked never works. Let's not forget that in 'charity' it is implicit that we should 'cherish': we can only do good to people if we love them – always with that benevolent divine neutrality. And if we love them, we need not be afraid of them. If we do not fear them, they will feel it and rejoice, contrary to what their provocative attitude might imply. Therefore, they will do us no harm. True generosity is about being completely devoid of fear before others. Love is an antidote to fear.

I know that this sounds like a fairy tale, and that there will always be violent louts, petty thieves ready to cut a finger off to grab a ring, bloodthirsty psychopaths and irresponsible and un-balanced people. But for goodness sake let's remember that this is not the rule, otherwise we will ourselves be drawn into the vicious circle of hatred and we will be able to do nothing to save ourselves, least of all humanity.

We need to expand that compassion, that Love which we need to survive, both individually and collectively, so that it encompasses the whole planet. And there again, we must repudiate false charity and the hypocrites who pretend they want to protect the planet. What do you think of those countries that sell arms and then mount rescue operations to alleviate their guilt, to make the world forget that they participated in the very crimes they denounce?

Better late than never, you will say. I am not one of those people who systematically criticize organized, high-profile charity events. If they help collect millions for a worthwhile cause, all the better. That we should be proud to have participated in such events is, however, rather questionable. Love must be reason enough in itself, and cannot be used to relieve guilt. Before becoming self-satisfied, we have to be effective. The main result of charity should be that it is useful.

Today, in a society which offers no meaning, many people, both young and old, dream of devoting themselves to humanitarian works. This can be laudable, as long as one is aware of the realities of such a romantic impulse. The specialists in humanitarian causes have to be careful regarding the true motivations of those who want to help. We shouldn't try to help the poor or homeless in a spirit of condescension. We should care for them as equals and in doing so help ourselves; by gathering our strengths and capabilities to do the work effectively, not by telling ourselves that we are 'doing good'. The nurse who works in a refugee camp in Africa does not think that she is doing good; she has neither the time nor the wish to think like that. She goes to those who need her most, and does her job within the context of that urgent and terrible reality.

In fact, one should not 'do' charity, but be compassionate, without any calculating ulterior motives – just the intention of really wanting to help others.

To do that we need something that goes beyond just charity. Charity is not enough to deal with the present world's confrontations. We should stop trying to reassure ourselves with these local appeasement policies and try to address the cause of these ills. What is the good of giving tuppence to a beggar, if behind his back we deplete his resources and ask him to pay back his debts, which we encouraged in the first place, and then finally rob him of his dignity? Why talk about development and mouth pious wishes for the improvement of Third-World countries, when we continue to squeeze more money out of them than we invest in them. Let's hope that Western leaders come to realize this soon, otherwise the great wars of the Apocalypse will come to pass.

Love is a real secret weapon, an inner law, and now represents the only way to avoid apocalyptic destruction. Humanity is treading a fine line between salvation and destruction. Its salvation lies in the passage into the Age of Aquarius, which holds the promise of universal reconciliation. Its destruction will come about if it does not learn to make use of love.

For love needs to be put into practice. The expression 'we are all brothers' all too often reflects an idealism in which, deep down, nobody believes. We prey on each other, and the time has come for this to stop. We need to face up to reality: the time has come to make a choice. Either we renounce violence altogether (whatever its nature), or we fall into the abyss. Good intentions are no longer enough; we have to put them into practice. 'But he who hears [my words] and does not do them is like a man who built a house on the ground without a foundation; against which the stream broke, and immediately it fell, and the ruin of that house was great' (Luke 6: 49).

That destruction lies in wait for us. The Bible warns us and Christ was very clear on the matter: 'Think not that I have come to abolish the law and the prophets; I have come not to abolish but to fulfil them'. (Matthew 5: 17)

We must be careful! We should not make the mistake of thinking that love which is spoken about in sweet terms is just empty piety. 'Behold, how good and pleasant it is when brothers dwell in unity,' says Psalm 133. 'For there the Lord has commanded the blessing, life for evermore.' I can hear all the sarcastic remarks! And yet, is this sweetness not preferable to our present barbaric state? We should be on the alert! Let's not forget that the Apocalypse closes the Bible, with its numerous potential torments. Apocalypse actually means 'revelation', but we will only receive this revelation if we radically change our ways. Love for the whole world has now become a necessity. Let's take advantage of the prayer of the heart, which brings us closer to God, to discover that love. 'He who does not love does not know God; for God is Love,' states I John 4: 8. That total love is not about sentimentality. It is not a mood, but a state of the soul, a strength and a necessity. Let's forget all the techniques to avoid solitude, fear, hatred, danger; we have to go beyond those to reach universal love. Without passion or desire for possession or profit, we now have to achieve 'neutral' love, which is far more generous; we will not be able to avoid going through this mutation.

We have used and abused Malraux's[15] famous saying, according to which 'the twenty-first century will be religious or it will not be', without truly realizing what it implies. Malraux was not announcing a future trend, a fashionable return to spirituality as one might predict the return of flared trousers or the hula-hoop. He was saying: 'Beware!' The important thing is the second part of the saying 'or it will not be'. This clearly means that if we do not find the true sense of the message contained in the sacred texts, of sharing and brotherhood, then humanity will inevitably flounder into annihilation and destruction. Either the world of the twenty-first century opens up to love or it will not survive . . .

So once again, it is about 'loving the world'. This is the most difficult kind of love for us to envisage, when we long to close our eyes to all that goes on in the world and fool ourselves that we are not responsible for our fellow human beings. We should remember Cain's terrible cry, after murdering Abel: 'Am I my brother's keeper?' Well, yes, we are our brothers' keepers! And God's reply is addressed to us: 'What have you done? The voice of your brother's blood is crying to me from the ground.' We know that Cain was spared, but his accursed descendants were wiped out by the Flood . . .

So it is up to us to act. The greatest proof of love which God can give us is, without doubt, to leave our free will intact. We remain the masters of our destiny and, consequently, we are responsible for the fate of our planet. It is up to us to choose which path to take. In His love, God would like to show us the way, but the final choice is ours. That is the meaning of God's question to Cain before the murder: 'Why are you angry, and why has your countenance fallen? If you do well, will you not be accepted? And if you do not do well, sin is crouching at the door; its desire is for you, but you must master it.'

Will we be able to tame our egotistical and self-centred tendencies? Will we manage to open our hearts? Will we lift our heads to contemplate, like the Sphinx of Guiza, the sun, that ray of divine light?

If we choose the right path – not necessarily the easiest – and if, after having made use of love, we learn to serve the Love which comes from God, that tremendous energy will save us from the torment of matter. Love thus conceived will be not only a source of joy, but also a fantastic journey which will lead us to explore higher thresholds. 'Love is strong as death,' says the Song of Solomon 6: 6. I would say that it is *stronger* that death, for it comes from God and leads us to Him. It's a 'fire brought to earth', so that human love may acquire a divine dimension. In this way our fellow men also represent our best path towards divinity. That love we carry within is our compass to help us find grace. It is no doubt for this reason that Christ says, in that famous gesture when he points to his heart chakra: 'This is the path that leads to my Father's kingdom.'

7

How Can We Find God?

❧✦❧

Being asked by the Pharisees when the kingdom of God
was coming, he answered them, 'The kingdom is not coming
with signs to be observed; nor will they say. "Lo, here
it is!" or "There!" for behold, the kingdom of God
is in the midst of you.'
LUKE 17: 20–21

Our spiritual quest and the meditative techniques we have practised help us feel increasingly aware of the immanent presence of God guiding us, sustaining us, sometimes overwhelming us, and yet the absolute dream remains: to perceive, if only for one moment, that presence, to feel with certitude (are we still in doubt?) that we have found God . . .

Some people have been fortunate enough to experience that illumination on the path to knowledge. Suddenly, divinity becomes visible and they are filled by a powerful radiance which awakens every cell of the body, blooming in the joy of infinite love. From the Sufi poems, through the Gnostic 'nuptial chamber', to the Song of Songs, all the great mystical texts have resorted to the language of love to express the ineffable merging with God.

To feel eternity in the present moment . . . That is how I would define closeness to God, if I did not know by experience that that proximity is indefinable. How is it possible to describe that prolonged vibration which is born within our heart, those shivers, that ecstasy which transports one into infinity and the great humility that one experiences?

At the risk of making the sceptics smile, I confess I have experienced that moment of revelation. In *Journey*, I recounted how, after many years of intense praying, when I least expected it, I felt that Light which changed my life. It did not happen in a holy place, but unexpectedly in the Pershing stadium in Vincennes. A luminous column appeared before me like a rainbow ripping the clouds, leaving me completely awe-struck. I felt in perfect harmony with the whole Cosmos, engulfed by the supreme Energy which animates all things, overwhelmed by the One. During that fragment of a second, I experienced eternity.

I can well imagine how such a confession might be irritating! You might allow for the ecstasies of St John of the Cross or St Teresa of Avila, because they seem the logical conclusion of a whole life dedicated to God. But that an ordinary person, albeit a 'believer' who prays a lot, should have such an experience, might well make you ask, 'Why him and not me?' Do not be so impatient; the moment will come if it is meant to, when you are ready for the perilous encounter with the Inexpressible. For if the veils of Isis mask the bright fire, it is not only to guide the initiate to a gradual discovery, but also to remind us that the Truth is blinding. Numerous traditions state that Divinity cannot be revealed to us, for it would mean risking 'disintegration' or madness.

In our Judaeo-Christian religion, God showed Himself on earth to Elijah and Enoch. Both were swallowed up by a column of fire, no ashes were left, and their whole being was transformed into pure energy. Thus we need first of all to contact the intermediaries who form the link between us and God. Those guardian angels and the celestial hierarchy are there for us, to reassure and guide us and help us on our way towards that ultimate union.

The path to God is not a desolate crossing of the desert, where only the arrival makes up for the trip. Waiting for ecstasy is punctuated by joy! As we progress in self-purification, as we clear our minds, each step we take brings a powerful explosion of joy. That kind of phenomenon can recur, acting as a kind of signpost to encourage you to carry on and help you to realize all you have achieved. Those celestial vibrations will descend to you, during meditation, every time you 'hit the right note'.

Don't focus on the final illumination. It is important to know that by putting yourself *really* on the path – not to reach a new state of consciousness, but to attain a higher knowledge – you will see that your transformation is happening little by little. Regular practice inevitably brings results. Even if you don't have a mystical experience, you will feel your daily worries fade away. To be more precise, it is the way you look at them which will change . . . You will become more detached, and see things from another point of view, from a higher perspective. But you must also take care. Your everyday difficulties may in fact be a warning.

We are now touching on a delicate subject, straying onto the theme of 'divine punishment'. However, this is not 'punishment' as such, but rather a reminder or a call to order. This is an important subtlety, which shows God's love and His desire to see us progress. Many of our disappointments bring us back to the reality of the path. So instead of feeling aggravated or irritated, why not learn to put those warnings to good use? If we can look differently at these small incidents, we become more responsible.

If you fail in something, might it be because you have neglected to give it due care and attention? If your child is tempted by drugs, is it perhaps because you have not been able to show him your love or show him that life can be happy? If you have a health problem, might it be because you have ignored your body for too long? Naturally, the links between events are not always so obvious or so direct, and are sometimes quite complex, but the principle remains the same: every affliction is a warning. But be careful: that does not authorize us to jump to conclusions regarding the problems of others. The destiny of others is always harder to understand than yours. So we should not be judgmental. As for ourselves, rather than angrily saying, 'Why me?', we should ask for divine help to show us the right way. You can even try praying forcefully: 'I am in a difficult situation, what should I do? I put myself in your hands, but please help me. Give me a sign!'

Once we begin to look at our difficulties from that angle, a miracle happens: things tend to smooth themselves out and the signs become clearer. Once I assume responsibility for myself things begin to develop in a way that never ceases to astound me. The more on edge you become about a problem, the more difficult it is to find a solution. If, on the other hand, you ask God's forgiveness with sincerity and trust, and if you honestly look to see where you've gone wrong and you act to mend your ways, then you will be shown how to solve the problem. And, little by little, from problem accepted to problem resolved, you will find your way to serenity.

Serenity . . . Don't you like the word? Well, you should. For the kind of serenity I am referring to has nothing to do with lukewarm indifference. It is a way of looking at the world, a wonderful way of approaching God. To achieve it, we must practise what I call 'maceration'. To obtain the philosopher's stone, the ultimate goal of this quest, the alchemist had first of all to put the *prima materia*, the antimony, into a mortar and then grind it finely in order to separate, according to Hermes Trismegistus, 'the subtle from the thick'. 'Maceration' represents that inner work which allows the heavy part of our being to settle, allowing the subtle part, the spirit, to elevate itself. False problems can then be distinguished from the real, the terrestrial from the celestial, the temporary from the eternal.

'Maceration' puts an end to the doubt we experience when, having read, gathered information and experienced, we still feel unable to make the connection between all these elements. We have understood certain points, but the synthesis and the understanding of the whole process is still missing. We have not yet grasped all the messages. That accumulated knowledge 'macerates' within us, as in an alembic, pounded by hope . . . And then suddenly, thanks to our meditation work, a light intervenes and a whole section of knowledge opens up in its full splendour. The way becomes clear and knowledge comes in its primordial simplicity, dissolving the apparent complexity of the world and human opinions.

We then become like the image of the archer found both in Japanese Zen and in Islam. He aims at the target, which is a metaphor for God. He takes his bow, his instrument, his philosophy; he stands well grounded, feet apart, overcomes his trembling, and positions the arrow. The tension of the string represents meditation, that ardent prayer made by the archer. But while the string is taut, he cannot reach God. One day, he looks at the target, at the arrow and his bow and tells himself that they are all one. He loosens his grip and the arrow goes right to the centre. It pierces the darkness of ignorance and establishes a direct link, a straight line, between the heart of the archer and the centre of the target, between the kernel of his being and the One. This is spiritual perfection, the perfect union about which the Muslim mystic Hallaj, known as 'the Christ of Islam' sings. His radical faith led him to being crucified in Baghdad in the ninth century.

> Between God and myself there are no more explanations
> nor proof nor signs to convince me.
> Behold the apparition of God radiates,
> flame-like within me, as an invaluable pearl.

To make this 'maceration' more efficient, and therefore to approach God more confidently, you can benefit from going on a retreat. This temporary escape is actually fashionable now, but there are many people who go about it in the worst possible way. They imagine that by spending two days in a convent or a monastery, they will benefit from God's grace and have time to think over their problems. As a spiritual proposition, this is almost insulting! You have worries? Try to find God where He really is and you will see that your cares fall into perspective.

If you do go on retreat, start by becoming aware of the space of your cell, be conscious of that prayer-stool, that crucifix or that icon which will remind you why you are there. Let the silence which reigns in such places envelop you. That silence which is in itself what the monastic rules call 'the great ceremony'. Take part in all the services, take advantage of the benefits that communal prayer brings. You're not there to analyze your existence or reflect on it, but only to situate yourself on a vibrational level, in the moment.

A retreat can help us understand that our daily problems are like aeroplanes crossing the sky; they may break the silence, draw a white line on the blue space, but the immense sky was there before and remains after their passage. We realize that the greatest secrets are always available to us but we pass them by, oblivious, distracted by the passing aeroplanes. When you are meditating on a text from the scriptures and the deeper sense of the words touches the heart of your being, you forget the outer world and you are filled with strength and joy.

It is not yet like seeing God, but that vibration-prayer rises to heaven and suddenly we take a great step forward. We know that God and His hierarchies are around us. We feel their presence, the caress of their breath or their encouraging laughter. For God is joy, you can be sure of that! As we have said before, the suffering of the saints and other martyrs took place to lighten the weight of our collective karma. But, if we agree to put ourselves in His care, God becomes synonymous with happiness. That indescribable bliss is an elixir which shields us from every danger. When we are contained by that Divine Love, the whole of the astral world leans towards us and whispers: 'Nothing can trouble you any longer.'

That is what the benefits of a retreat are like, but there is more to it than that. If you have understood the lesson properly, you will be capable of 'going into a retreat' anywhere, be it your house in the country or a consecrated place of worship. Perhaps one day suspending our normal activities will become unnecessary for we will have learned how to prolong that state of retreat indefinitely . . .

Are those who cannot attain that supreme serenity aware that the secret lies in completely letting go? All religions insist on this necessary passage towards Divinity, whatever name it is given: capitulation, annihilation, surrender, renunciation, abandonment, obedience . . . The very word Islam means 'submission'. This notion lends itself to many misunderstandings. We take it to mean submission to rites and dogma, whereas it is about submitting to the divine will. Far from being a defeat, it is our most beautiful victory! It does not condemn us to servile apathy, but throws us into the great river of life. It does not ask us to accept bondage, but on the contrary, it allows us to put down our burden! To let go means to stop tensing up uselessly, and to let yourself be supported. Whereas we behave like a ridiculous traveller who still insists on lugging his baggage around on board ship . . .

We have to admit that there is nothing more difficult than completely letting go. It comes down to accepting everything that happens to us as the expression of God's Love for us and as His desire to show us the way. It means much more than allowing ourselves to ponder our life's petty worries; it means fearlessly welcoming illness, old age and death. The contemporary idea that these three things have to be kept out of the way and concealed is very revealing. Those who are ill or old are put in quarantine, not for their own comfort, but so as not to upset the rest of us. We hide away the dying, and we bury people at dawn, surreptitiously and quickly. It is obvious that it is our non-acceptance of old age and death that stops us from being happy. This knee-jerk reaction makes us eager for power, for riches and for pleasures, as if to compensate us for our panic-stricken fear. A vain effort, seeing that our time here on earth is so brief . . .

We are at such a loss that when our dead have left this life, we only acknowledge them when we want to call for their help. We ask them to show us supernatural tricks, or beg for moral support, which as I have already said we should not do. 'Let the dead bury the dead,' Christ said brutally. A deceased soul is plunged into an energetic universe, where it slowly makes its way through several thresholds to reach heaven. What right have we to interrupt that ascension? To cry for our dead is a crime; we should instead 'laugh with our dead'! Rather than trying to hold them back, we should be saying, 'Don't lose your way, ascend towards God and our joy will be all the more intense.'

We should be careful that our interest in spirituality is not just another veil to mask our fear of old age and death. Nobody can prove God's existence, or the theory of reincarnation, but when our conviction comes from *experience*, we know that we are not just looking for comfort for our fear of death, as the cynics would have us believe. We do not deny the existence of suffering or misfortune, we simply stop placing these in irreconcilable conflict with life.

One of the most revealing passages of the Bible is the following sentence from Job 2: 10: 'Shall we receive good at the hand of God, and shall we not receive evil?' while the *Tao Te Ching* says: 'Misfortune brings good fortune, good fortune must precede misfortune.'

Throughout time man has searched for happiness. However, that quest has brought about some terrible misunderstandings. We have hoped for permanent happiness, and an end to all un-pleasantness. This has led to the great mistakes of our civilization: we have confused happiness with accumulation of wealth and material comfort. We have to be careful not to fall under the spell of another fantasy, namely looking for happiness in spiritual escapism. A spiritual quest is not about running away from reality: it is a long path *towards* reality. We need to understand that our dualist conceptions, separating good and evil, rational and irrational, happiness and unhappiness, merely expose us to con-tinual dilemmas and frustrations. I don't deny the existence of happiness, but I do prefer, for clarity's sake, the term serenity, for true happiness means taking misfortune into consideration.

'Your will be done, not mine!' No initiate or adept can pretend to know what that will is. We have to accept it, whatever it may be, knowing that it will be good for us. Once again, this is not fatalism: on the contrary, it is a question of coming to grips not with 'what should be', but with 'what is', so we can bounce back into life and into the present.

That attitude is the only valid one from a logical point of view. Why exhaust ourselves swimming against the current, when we can swim with it. 'Who can resist God's will and remain at peace?' asks Job. By abandoning ourselves to divine will, we do not suffer humiliation; we learn acceptance which brings us closer to God.

Far from being a simple technique, meditation of the heart little by little permeates our way of looking at life. Prayer becomes a state and our life becomes a prayer. 'Think of God more often than you breathe,' said Epictetus[16]. After the prayer-litany, the prayer-request for help, and the prayer of the heart, we are ready for the prayer-adoration, the dazzling call to Divinity.

Do not think that perpetual prayer is reserved for the contemplative orders. Do not deprive yourself of it, under the pretext of a lack of time. God does not take up any time, since He is always present! We work, we eat, we discuss, and prayer continues. When I breathe in, I pray; when I breathe out, I still pray. Thus we manage to make breathing an act of adoration. To think of God is not to lose oneself in theological arguments; it's simply to live in awareness of His presence.

When the Virgin Mary, in her recent apparitions, urges us to halt humanity's mad rush towards destruction, encouraging us to 'become beings of prayer', she is not asking us just to dedicate a quarter of an hour of our time to vague incantations, but rather to become a new type of person, able to look at the world with renewed understanding, seeing a unified whole. The soul who, as the Gnostics say, can state that 'it has acquired self-knowledge and collected its dispersed parts', has surmounted the complexity of the world and the fragmentation of the self, as well as the dualisms which cause such stress! Even the traditional opposition between active and contemplative life is effaced.

'Blessed are the unified ones and the elect: for they will find the Kingdom. They came from it and will return to it,' says the apocryphal Gospel of Thomas (logion 49). The Greek text reads 'blessed are the *monachos*'; these are not just 'monks', but all who have been able to recover their primordial wholeness.

That same book (logion 22) describes that wholeness in an image of childlike simplicity, revealing it as the secret which will allow us to merge with God:

> Jesus saw little ones who suckled at the breast.
> He told his disciples: 'Those little ones who suckle
> are like those who enter into the Kingdom.'
> They asked him:
> 'So, by becoming little, we will enter into the Kingdom?'
> Jesus told them:
> 'When you have made of the two One
> and that the interior will be as the exterior,
> and the exterior as the interior,
> the high as the low,
> when you have made masculine and feminine
> one Unity,
> when you have eyes in your eyes,
> a hand in your hand,
> and a foot in your foot,
> and an icon in your icon,
> then you will enter into the Kingdom!'

That unity is what we have been searching for from the beginning of our quest: to resist the fragmentation of the mind, to regain the harmony between body and spirit, to reconcile the social individual with the spiritual being, to rediscover unity with the Cosmos, to find solidarity in brotherhood . . . a vast work of reunification which will, perhaps, be rewarded with merging with God.

That unity is something we crave so much, and we would dearly like to see it put into practice by the churches, but fanaticism and loss of identity are on the increase everywhere.

In these pages I have frequently referred to the religious texts of the major religions, choosing to limit these references to the Judaeo-Christian, the Muslim and the Oriental traditions. From these we have taken some practical exercises, to show how while the exterior form and the ritualistic ceremonies might vary, the purpose is the same – to ensure our well-being and our salvation. In short, we are continually brought face to face with the proof that the major religions, in essence, come together. Yet, in spite of this, we see 'religious' people everywhere tearing each other apart, fighting for the supremacy of their faith, for the most part verbally, but sometimes with weapons. Instead of uniting against war and hatred, today's religions are more often than not the pretext, the catalyst or the cause of war.

Even if I recognize a particular religion as my own, because it corresponds to the civilization into which I incarnated, should I necessarily reject all the others as mistaken and false? That problem which has, for a long time, been debated by theologians and atheists has now become a major issue for world peace.

In order to resolve these conflicts, we should first of all distinguish between the 'historical' official churches and the message that they are supposed to transmit, which they twist unashamedly, under the pretext of proselytism. From that wide gap between institution and inspiration, the most terrible misunderstandings arise. Who could really agree that the true message of Islam is contained in some of the radical positions of today? How can we see the values of Catholicism in movements such as the Inquisition or Irish separatism? Does Oriental wisdom encourage the murderous combats between the Sikhs and the Hindus? Judaeo-Christianity, which we like to consider as being on the side of the poor, has long been the accomplice of Western colonialism. Religions seem unable to resist the desire for domination and prestige . . .

Fortunately, the initiate learns early on to take a detached view of these secular caricatures. He knows how to recognize those who try to put his quest at the service of such manipulative ideals. The apocryphal Gospel of Peter warns us to be careful of those who 'give themselves the title of bishop or deacon as if God had given them their authority. They bend under the judgment of their superiors. Those people are dried-up channels.' In other words, the current of supreme energy no longer flows through them. They have lost the keys to the Kingdom.

Religious fanatics of any kind are like the observers who were sent by a prince into a darkened room to give him a description of an elephant which had just been captured. The first touched the trunk and described the animal as a long sinuous serpent; the second one, who hit a leg, spoke of a sturdy column, whereas the third, who felt the elephant's flank described a large rugged surface . . . By limiting ourselves to our partial perceptions, we obviously reach a point of unyielding opposition – without realizing that we are talking about the same thing! The one God, the Truth, which every religion approaches in its own way. So why fight each other to decide which religion (which are by nature imperfect because made by human beings) is the best and serves God in the correct manner? Why not consult the words of the great initiates and the great mystics? Whatever their faith, they never ceased to preach universal tolerance.

The enlightened spirits do, in fact, understand that by denigrating an unfamiliar creed, one ends up discrediting one's own, restricting it in a sectarian way. In the third century before Jesus Christ, the great Indian and Buddhist emperor Asoka had the following inscription engraved on a rock, still legible today: 'One should not just honour one's own religion and condemn that of others, but one should respect other religions. Whoever honours their own religion and condemns that of others, does it out of devotion, thinking "I shall glorify my religion". But on the contrary, by acting thus, he does damage to it. Therefore, an understanding is advisable: may everyone listen and be willing to hear the doctrines of other religions.'

Faced with the growth of fundamentalism, what a comfort it is to hear Buddha, the founder of one of the most important schools of thought, declare: 'It is not advisable for a man who supports Truth to conclude: "This is the Truth and the rest is false"'!

Why is it that verse 68 of the fifth Sura of the Koran is hardly ever mentioned? It tells how Mohammed extended a hand to Jews and Christians by exorting the adepts of those faiths thus: 'You who have received the Scriptures, you will be in the wrong as long as you do not behave according to the Torah and to the Scriptures and to all that has been revealed to you by your Lord'. For the faithful know that 'God is our Lord and your Lord. We have our deeds, and you have your deeds . . . God shall bring us together, and unto Him is the homecoming' (Sura 42: 15).

In professing such universalism, some Sufi masters incurred the wrath of their official religion and were accused of heresy. The same is true for numerous mystics who, after an intuitive experience or revelation dared to state that they preferred no religion in particular.

Once the initiate is sufficiently advanced, he can cultivate a certain detachment regarding current religious practices. His aim is to experience an inner reality, and so his quest goes beyond conventional practice. He seeks nourishment in the 'Word' at various levels. Meister Eckhart[17] said, 'If you want the kernel, you must pierce the shell.' The important thing is to continue evolving and seeking the hidden meaning of the sacred texts, whatever religion we were brought up in. This was expressed very poetically by the great master of Muslim esotericism, Ibn Arabi (1165–1240 CE): 'My heart is capable of adopting many forms: the Christian monk's cloister, a temple for idols, a prairie for gazelles, the pilgrims' black stone, Moses' Tablets, the Koran . . . Love is my belief and my faith.'

One of his contemporaries, the famous poet-apothecary Attar (1142–1220 CE), wrote *The Language of the Birds*, a story in which the diversity of birdsong is used to suggest the variety of ways in which one can approach God. Not content with preaching tolerance, he actually foresees a return to unity: 'I am certain that tomorrow the seventy-two sects will be but one. Why should I say that this one is bad, that one is good, since if you observe them well, they are all searching for the Supreme Being? Oh Lord, may our hearts worship only You and keep the fanatic far away from You.'

Today, that path towards unity and religious reconciliation is not the privilege of enlightened beings. There was a time, it is true, when religions kept secrets which were not to be revealed to those of other faiths. Contact between different religions was rare, even forbidden, whereas today any Christian can find out as much as he wants about Judaism, or about Oriental and Muslim religions. St Augustine said: 'I mistrust the man who follows the teachings of one single book.' We can show our curiosity and, without necessarily becoming experts in comparative religion, substitute our rejection of other faiths with a desire for understanding through keeping an open mind. If you really believe in the existence of an only God, a God of Love, do you think that He worries in what language prayers are expressed? Or whether you present yourself before Him sitting down, kneeling or wearing a suit? Do you really imagine that God would prefer one cult or ritual to another?

Far from being just desirable, this enlarged ecumenical community has become a necessity. Any other way will lead to confrontation. We know that behind every conflict there are cultural, religious and economic interests. Dialogue between all the different religions is, therefore, urgent. It is the best way of finding a way of living harmoniously with our neighbours in this global village of ours.

The second Vatican Council took a step, albeit rather timidly and theoretically, in the right direction. In the early 1960s, for the first time, it discreetly recognized the value of other religions: 'From ancient times up to the present, we find among the different peoples a certain sensitivity to the hidden force which is present at the heart of things and events in human life, at the same time as a recognition of the existence of a supreme Divinity, or even of the Father.' But how much progress has been made since then, in terms of dialogue between the various religions? What we are asking of these different parties is nothing more than actually putting their message of peace into practice.

In fact, each of us should now realize that the separation between true and false is no longer a question of a difference between faiths; each creed has to deal with that problem by studying its own history. We need to be able to recognize what features in our rituals, in our dogmas and even in certain of our sacred texts, result from their historical context, rather than being a revelation of the Truth. It is now important to separate what is written and what is spiritual experience, what is exoteric and what is esoteric . . .

Such a reading would renew the spirit of the sacred texts, giving them new life and no doubt a universal religion would be born, as announced by all the prophecies. Such an evolution is implicit in the unfolding cycle of human history. Each new era has its own morality. Man has thus successively known the religion of the Taurean Age, based on sacrifice, that of the Ram, founded on justice, and finally that of Pisces, the promised era of love. The Age of Aquarius will be the time of love made real. No more pious or pompous ostentation, nor the imposed dogmas of our present religions. In Haggai 2: 9 we can read: 'The latter splendour of this house shall be greater than the former, says the Lord of hosts; and in this place I will give peace.' A natural morality will have substituted the morality of duty.

We can say no more about this future religion, except that it will be both radical and yet a marked return to primordial sources. All heritage is metamorphosis, says the philosopher . . . But how are we going to arrive at the metamorphosis?

Perhaps we should recall the famous biblical story of Hiram, the master mason. King Solomon was haunted by the desire to build a temple in which he could serve God with dignity. Unable to build it himself, he called the master mason Hiram, nicknamed the 'transfigured one', who possessed inner strength and the secrets of construction. If today's churches want to help us and themselves out of our present impasse, they will definitely have to accept the guidance of esoteric mysticism. For a long time, religion has insisted on rejecting mysticism as being folly and esotericism as obscure. By waging war against alternative ways of approaching God, conventional religion wanted to preserve its power over men. In reality, esotericism and mysticism seek to discover the hidden meaning of the sacred texts and their inner significance, as opposed to the outer form. Far from being dangerous deviations, these movements could well constitute the safeguard needed to prevent us from succumbing to fundamentalism.

The great initiates have always known how to establish links between the different traditions for mutual enrichment. They have preserved true knowledge, the 'lost word'. There have been some privileged meeting points, where all these traditions have met. Egypt was one of them, where the wisdom from the lost civilization of Atlantis, Hermeticism and the Sufi tradition all mingled. Persia was another, where contact with the Zoroastrian and Hindu traditions was established, and where Christian and Muslim brotherhoods learned yoga breathing techniques. Spain, of course, was where the alchemists were inspired by Arab scholars and by the Jewish Cabbalists, authors of the *Zohar*. Two great mystics were born there, often compared though from completely different cultures – the Sufi Ibn Arabi and the Christian St John of the Cross. One could write whole volumes on the extraordinary interlacing of these various influences, thanks to which the spark of the sacred fire was preserved and is now ready to be rekindled.

The Church has always considered Christian esotericism as being anathema, and has thus marginalized it. Buddhism did not make that mistake and has always sought to enrich itself by cultivating its mystical currents, Zen and Tao. Islam itself, despite certain periodic tensions, has never cut itself off from Sufism.

Whatever happens, we can be sure that the religion of the coming Age of Aquarius will draw on the living forces of the spirit and not on literal interpretation of the scriptures.

'There shall be one flock, one shepherd,' John 10: 16 tells us, speaking of the new era. Nevertheless, we have to be careful not fall into naive syncretism, when we think of the world as a global village. When I speak of an all-encompassing ecumenical attitude, I do not mean that we should not take into consideration the unique qualities of every religion. It is a question of creating 'inner' bridges, which will allow for communication between Christians, Muslims or Buddhists or members of other faiths, without effacing their particular characteristics.

When St Augustine said that he mistrusted the man who followed the teachings of just a single book, he was warning us both against the dangers of fundamentalism and of 'totalitarian' religions. And if I advocate a universal religion, that does not mean I am calling for the disappearance of today's numerous beliefs, with their individual characteristics. I am saying – and this is extremely ambitious – that we should aim at establishing a consensus between faiths and between men, both on a spiritual and on a personal level. Religions, with their individual character-istics, would then be like windows of different shapes opening onto the same sky or, even better, like the colours which make up the spectrum, emanating from one sole light source.

The myth of the tower of Babel warns against dreaming of a single culture, on the surface favourable to world peace, and against us working to achieve the realization of such a project. That seems to be the great temptation now, a global and uniform civilization . . . But God put an end to that crazy project by creating a multiplicity of languages. The Bible could not have chosen a clearer way of telling us that creating a totalitarian regime as a solution to all our problems is a perverse idea, created by our pride and our tendency to go to extremes. Both people and religions have to become conscious that we are all 'similar, but different': only then will our broader ecumenical attitude become the basis for meeting, exchange and mutual enrichment.

Unfortunately, we are forced to admit that we are very far from that. On the rare occasions when dialogue is encouraged, it is immediately crushed by the old reflex of tensing up before an adversary. Now that we are almost at the end of the Kali-Yuga era, the age of growing darkness, we are obviously still not ready for reconciliation, hence confrontation reigns everywhere. Yet it is time we reacted against this trend. Remember that the proliferation of religious sects is one of the first signs of the Apocalypse. But we don't know how to interpret these signs . . .

Nevertheless, the signs are there for those who want to see them. In 1993, American astronomers detected an object, a comet, heading towards Jupiter. They named it Shoemaker-Levy, adding the number 9 as it was their ninth discovery. In 1994 this comet hit Jupiter's surface. In fact, it had already fragmented into 22 asteroids, forming a curious necklace of cosmic pearls. The impacts, of surprising violence, were easily observable from the earth.

For anyone who is familiar with the language of the Cabbalah, the message is clear. The shoemaker is, together with the fish, the symbol of Christ, who washes the feet of his disciples, as if to purify them of their false steps. The 'shoemaker' thus announces the closing of the Piscean Age. Levi was the third son of Jacob and Leah, and therefore the ancestor of the 12 tribes of Israel. The 'sons of Levi' are presented in the Bible as the guarantors of the descendance of that tribe, who chastized those who worshipped the Golden Calf, who would transmit the teaching of the Law . . .

Shoemaker-Levy 9 . . . Strangely enough, nine is the perfect number, $3 \times 3 = 9$, the sacred Pythagorean ennead, the number of God the Father, whom we also find symbolized by Jupiter, the Greek Zeus, the sovereign power which creates thunder. As for the 22 asteroids, which evoke the 22 major arcana cards in the Tarot, these have been demolished and the alchemical Work is finished. In other words, the cycle of Pisces is coming to an end and this, having been decreed by God, is being announced to us by 'the sons of Levi', those who struck at God's offenders. We have now entered that terrifying moment which Christ called 'the end of time' and of which the Revelation of St John says: 'These times will be so hard that for love of you I will shorten them.' We are living in accelerated times, the moment of direct karma: mistakes will no longer be paid for from one life to the next, but instantaneously.

'At the end of time,' the Virgin told us in one of her recent apparitions, 'there will be visible signs everywhere.' Everyone across the word was able to watch, through a telescope or on television, the collision of Shoemaker-Levy 9's fragments with Jupiter . . . Is this the comet mentioned in the prophecies, that 'hairy star' come to send us a last warning? Nobody seemed very worried by this phenomenon. 'They will have eyes to see and they will not, they will have ears to hear and they will not . . .'

We are entering into a period of great confusion, and we are going to be faced with a vast cataclysm, with 'God's three days of wrath'. It seems that the inhabitants of Gaia will have to go through these apocalyptic tribulations before contemplating universal reconciliation. Then it will become clear that all fanaticism is foolish and fundamentalism, incapable of dealing with the urgency of the situation, will be exposed.

Our hope is that an external event of terrible proportions, an event which I perceive as coming not from the earth but from heaven, like that comet, will force all humankind, under the threat of extinction, to come together and pray. All the old antagonisms will melt like snow in the sun before this planetary peril. People will really be made to feel the fear that humanity may die out and thus experience the brotherhood of the whole human race.

Hence everything will be possible: freed from all selfishness and from every material obsession, human conscience will be able to change for the better and modify the course of things. Universal prayer has, as the Bible tells us, the power to move mountains. Why might it not change the course of an asteroid? Let us remember the words of hope conveyed by the Virgin, when she appeared in Kerizinen, in Brittany, in 1948: 'Soon, when the historians look for the event which changed the face of the world, which brought peace and prosperity, they will discover that it was not a battle, but a prayer.'

Faced with such urgency and such huge responsibility, we must not fall into the trap of solitary discouragement. On the contrary, we have at least two excellent reasons to reinforce our vigilance and the diligence which guides our personal quest. First of all, because in these 'last times' we are also blessed: for the first time, souls have the possibility of a quicker ascent to higher energy levels, and to gain access to divine illumination in the space of one lifetime.

The second reason is that the scale of the violence with which the transition into the Age of Aquarius occurs will depend on how successful our quest is; it will be proportional to our degree of spiritual elevation. By the use we make of our free will, we can influence the tribulations to come. Let us try to increase the number of the just, the just who would have enabled Sodom and Gomorrah to be spared, if only a handful of them had been found (Genesis 18).

Whatever happens we must know that our journey is not towards final destruction, but a return to God. 'Everything has come from the Unity, so shall everything return to it in similar fashion,' said Jacob Boehme in *De Signatura Rerum*. Except that it will depend on our free will. Everything that is degenerate here on earth, imprisoned by the dense world of matter, can seek to return to its divine source, but to do so we must endeavour to perform a task of universal reintegration, of regeneration both of ourselves as individuals and of the whole Cosmos. That is the ultimate aim of the alchemists who, through their work, seek to bring about the transmutation of matter, the metamorphosis which will save humanity by allowing it to pass to a higher energy level.

In the same way, if the initiate has chosen the narrow path, if the faithful do good around them, it is neither for their personal glory nor to secure a place in paradise. Their actions and their observance of the divine commandments will spread beneficial waves around us. Isaiah 58: 9–12 fills us with hope, proclaiming the healing effect of our Work:

> If you take away from the midst of you the yoke,
> the pointing of the finger, and speaking wickedness,
> if you pour yourself out for the hungry
> and satisfy the desire of the afflicted,
> then shall your light rise in the darkness
> and your gloom be as the noonday.
> And the Lord will guide you continually,
> and satisfy your desire with good things,
> and make your bones strong;
> and you shall be like a watered garden,
> like a spring of water,
> whose waters fail not.
> And your ancient ruins shall be rebuilt;
> you shall raise up the foundations of many generations;
> you shall be called the repairer of the breech,
> the restorer of streets to dwell in.

Humanity badly needs those 'repairers of the breech' now! Not only does it need saints and avatars who can absorb the forces of evil like black holes in space, but it needs people who, in themselves, in their families, at work, in their neighbourhood, are once more at peace with the world around them. People who, having silenced the ego, know how to comfort others and are a healing influence among the reigning external confusion. From being a hostile and chaotic place, our universe could then become a haven of peace. We must not expect the miracle to happen from outside, but from within ourselves. By seeking internal harmony we are not turning away from what is happening elsewhere; we are providing the strength to relieve the confusion which reigns in the outer world. Hermes Trismegistus wrote in his *Corpus Hermeticus* (I, 31–32): 'Fill me with strength, O God, Father of all things . . . So that I may enlighten with that grace all those of my race who live in ignorance, my brothers and my children.' St Seraphim[18] said the same: 'Acquire inner peace and a multitude of men will find salvation after you.' The Buddhist *Dhammapada* indicates that 'even a young monk who consecrates himself to the Doctrine of the Enlightened One will illuminate the world like the moon emerging from the clouds.'

Yes, we can escape that apocalyptic fate, which we thought we were powerless to alter. Then what will remain of the Apocalypse will be its original meaning: the revelation of a better world. God makes the following promises in Isaiah 65: 16–17, 25: 'former troubles are forgotten and are hid from my eyes. For behold, I create new heavens and a new earth . . . the lion shall eat straw like the ox . . . They shall not hurt or destroy in all my holy mountain.'

Make no mistake about it, the work we have accomplished so far is not a simple cosmetic job. The urge to participate in the evolution of the Cosmos, to participate in the end of the present cycle, to rise to higher energy levels and fulfil our karma, is a true revolution in which everything will change. Every era has to endure change, but we are being confronted with a very steep curve and the changes which await us are huge. It is our task to be worthy and to merit them.

The Age of Aquarius will mean a drastic change in attitudes. We will go forth from the Third to the Fourth Vibrational Level, so that our transfiguration and our renaissance can then occur. We are at the bottom of the abyss at present and we have two choices – either to disappear into that vortex, or to be reborn, transformed and strengthened by a new consciousness. That challenge is with us here and now, it cannot be put off for a distant and Utopian future. It belongs to the present, to the short time we have before the millennium, to the transition we are experiencing from one era to another.

To accept that challenge, we have at our disposal the techniques which I have described: meditation and prayer. Once again, it is through the help of these daily practices that changes become reality and not through our good intentions. It is through constant practice that you will gain the necessary strength to face the times to come and to revel in the joy of the present moment.

Finally, during that journey, even if you do not encounter God, you will discover, to your surprise, that you have acquired what some people call *faith*, which is none other than *trust*. That confidence which banishes fear and stress forever. That assurance which is, perhaps, true happiness. That trust we put in God's will is also the certainty that God grants us the independence to act according to our conscience.

If we are still afraid of not having the strength to lift ourselves towards Him, we can be reassured: He will come to meet us halfway. For God does not take a malicious pleasure in concealing himself. He does not even expect to be discovered, only sought out. In the *Bhagavad-Gita* (18: 65) we find these words: 'Fill your thoughts with Me, become My lover and My worshipper, prostrate yourself before Me, and to Me you will come. It is the assurance and the promise I make thee, for you are dear to Me.' The Sufi Ibn Arabi says: 'God comes to you in so far as you go to Him.' In his *Thoughts*, Pascal reassures us: 'Be comforted, you would not look for Me if you had not already found Me.'

Strengthened and with that certainty in your heart, do not worry about achieving perfection. Forget your dreams of illumination, and go forward in the present, without fear of the unknown, and do not build castles in the air, but know in your heart that when the time comes, God will recognize his own.

For the moment, work without respite at cultivating your inner treasure, and bring forth its fruits. Cultivate your inner paradise. For everything is there within you. Always remember: you are the temple, the altar and the celebrant.

Notes

Introduction

1 Paul Valéry (1871–1945). French philosophical poet.

Chapter 1

2 Blaise Pascal (1623–1662). French mathematician and philosopher.
3 Alain, pseudonym of French philosopher Emile Chartier (1868–1951).
4 Louis-Claude de Saint-Martin (1743–1803). French philosopher, theosophist and writer.

Chapter 2

5 St John Climacus (570–649). Ascetic and writer, Abbot of the monastery at Mount Sinai.
6 Emile Coué (1857–1926). French pharmacist and psychologist who developed a method of healing by auto-suggestion.

Chapter 3

7 The Essenes. A Jewish sect of around the time of Christ, which advocated poverty and asceticism. It has been suggested that both Jesus and John the Baptist might have been members of the Essene sect.
8 Pierre Corneille (1606–1684). French dramatist.

Chapter 4

9 Allan Kardec was a famous spiritualist, and the founder of an esoteric movement.

10 St Francis of Sales (1567–1622). French-born Bishop of Geneva. One of the leaders of the Counter-Reformation. Wrote instructions for devotional living.

11 Monsignor Gaillot is a bishop who believes in direct action and takes part in civil protests.

Chapter 5

12 Jacob Boehme (1575–1624). German mystic, a shoemaker by trade.

13 *Hyle* is the Greek word for matter. The Gnostics believed that spirit was essentially good, and that anything physical was essentially evil.

14 Gérard de Nerval, pen name of Gérard Labrunie (1808–1855). French symbolist and surrealist writer.

Chapter 6

15 André Malraux (1901–1976). French novelist and politician.

Chapter 7

16 Epictetus (50–130CE). Stoic philosopher. Originally a slave of the Emperor Nero, he was given his freedom and went on to become a renowned teacher and religious thinker.

17 Meister Eckhart (1260–1327). German Dominican mystic. Condemned by the Catholic Church as a heretic.

18 Seraphim of Sarov (1759–1833). Russian ascetic monk who lived much of his life as a hermit. He became a spiritual teacher, emphasizing the benefits of living joyfully with moderation.

Index

INDEX